Praise for
The Middle Matters

"I want to give Lisa-Jo's book a standing ovation because it's exactly what's needed for this particular time, when our 'ordinary' lives seem so unextraordinary compared with what we see or hear on our phones."
—AARTI SEQUEIRA, chef, TV personality, journalist, and author

"Through personal stories about love, loss, and life in the middle, Lisa-Jo invites us to take a long look inside our own mind's secret nooks and crannies, which aren't nearly as dark, scary, or ordinary as we might think."
—LAYLA PALMER, *The Lettered Cottage* blog

"In a world that is telling every woman to speed up and get to the good part or slow down because she's about to miss it, I'm so grateful a message like *The Middle Matters* is bringing the grace and truth and good news that we need."
—JESS CONNOLLY, author of *Wild and Free*

"This is the kind of book you will want to read once a year, simply to get a refresh on all the truths and practical ideas contained inside."
—MANDY ARIOTO, president and CEO of MOPS International

"For any adult who still sometimes feels like the shy, insecure kid from junior high, Lisa-Jo Baker is the breath of fresh air you've been waiting for. She gives us permission to fully embrace our lives—imperfections and all."
—JENNIFER FULWILER, SiriusXM radio host and author

"As someone who wakes up shocked most days that I'm middle aged but with young kids, I related to every word that Lisa-Jo put in this book. I read it in my messy car in the car line while I begrudgingly pulled out my new bifocals This is a story of every woman at some point in time."
—KELLY STAMPS, blogger and mom of three

"This incredible book is like a magic mirror. It showed me just how marvelous my ordinary life already is."
—CHRISTIE PURIFOY, author of *Placemaker* and cohost
of the *Out of the Ordinary* podcast

"With Lisa-Jo's guts as our unfettered guide, may we finally learn the sumptuous truth of our years: that a grilled cheese sandwich without the middle is just toast."

—ERIN LOECHNER, founder of OtherGoose.com and author of *Chasing Slow*

"In this witty and heartwarming book, Lisa-Jo Baker makes a case for why the middle matters. And just like an Oreo wouldn't be the same without the cream in the middle, those seemingly mundane and messy middle years can actually be where some of the best stuff of life happens!"

—CRYSTAL PAINE, founder of MoneySavingMom.com, host of *The Crystal Paine Show*, and *New York Times* best-selling author

"Lisa-Jo Baker isn't afraid to write what we're all thinking. She tackles middle age with her trademark wit and down-to-earth charm, making every reader feel like she's sitting on the other side of the table for a coffee chat with the author."

—COURTNEY WALSH, *New York Times* and *USA Today* best-selling author of *Things Left Unsaid*

"Lisa-Jo reveals that the seemingly ordinary points of life are what hold the meaning and beauty of our interwoven stories."

—JESSICA HONEGGER, Noonday Collection founder and author of *Imperfect Courage*

"No one writes about motherhood, marriage, and life as Lisa-Jo Baker does. *The Middle Matters* is a vulnerable, compelling read that I want to gift to every friend I know."

—JESSICA TURNER, best-selling author of *The Fringe Hours* and *Stretched Too Thin*

"Thank you, Lisa-Jo, for reminding women everywhere how important it is to find meaning in the midst of the confusing middle."

—JOY PROUTY, artist and educator

"In *The Middle Matters,* Lisa-Jo gives us all a motivational mission and a plan for making it happen. Here's to finding glory in the middle!"

—CLAIRE DIAZ-ORTIZ, author and speaker

The Middle Matters

Why That (Extra)Ordinary Life
Looks Really Good on You

LISA-JO
BAKER

BEST-SELLING AUTHOR
OF *NEVER UNFRIENDED*

WATERBROOK

THE MIDDLE MATTERS

Hardcover ISBN 978-0-52565-284-7
eBook ISBN 978-0-52565-285-4

Copyright © 2019 by Lisa-Jo Baker

Cover design by Mark D. Ford; cover photo by Amy Hinman; author bio photo by Chelsea Hudson–Storyographer

The author is represented by Alive Literary Agency, 7680 Goddard Street, Suite 200, Colorado Springs, Colorado, 80920, www.aliveliterary.com.

Published in the United States by WaterBrook, an imprint of the Crown Publishing Group, a division of Penguin Random House LLC, New York.

WATERBROOK® and its deer colophon are registered trademarks of Penguin Random House LLC.

Library of Congress Cataloging-in-Publication Data
Names: Baker, Lisa-Jo, author.
Title: The middle matters : why that (extra)ordinary life looks really good on you/ Lisa-Jo Baker.
Description: First Edition. | Colorado Springs : WaterBrook, 2019.
Identifiers: LCCN 2018043833| ISBN 9780525652847 (hardcover) | ISBN 9780525652854 (electronic)
Subjects: LCSH: Middle-aged women—Religious life.
Classification: LCC BV4527 .B335 2019 | DDC 248.8/43—dc23
LC record available at https://lccn.loc.gov/2018043833

Printed in the United States of America
2019—First Edition

10 9 8 7 6 5 4 3 2 1

SPECIAL SALES
Most WaterBrook books are available at special quantity discounts when purchased in bulk by corporations, organizations, and special-interest groups. Custom imprinting or excerpting can also be done to fit special needs. For information, please e-mail specialmarketscms@penguin randomhouse.com or call 1-800-603-7051.

This book is for my mom, Jo Rous.

We lost her in the middle. But not before she taught me that the harder the moment, the greater the story.

Contents

Part 5: *Why the Middle of Your Failures Matters*

Part 6: *Why the Middle of All Those Sports Practices Matters*

Part 7: *Why the Middle of Your Friendships Matters*

Part 8: *Why the Middle of Your Faith Matters*

Welcome to the Middle!

*O*nce upon a time, I had no idea what a muffin top was. That time, my friend, has long passed. I'm in my forties now, and me and my muffin top—that chubby little bulge of tummy that refuses to stay tucked away behind the top button of my jeans but insists on grinning around at the world over the top of my waistband— are on the closest of terms. Maybe more so than I would like.

It is one of the landmarks of my middle. Literally. And metaphorically. Because when I bump up against that chunky midsection that I'm trying to accept, it's with the same surprise I feel late at night after I've exhausted another day of being in charge of my own life and the lives of all these people who live in our house, plus the cats.

I keep waiting to feel like a grown-up while going through all the grown-up motions. I'm not sure if these are the things you're supposed to say out loud. But isn't it weird to have all the responsibilities of a grown-up and look like a grown-up and have a grown-up job and a grown-up mortgage and still not be sure how or when to change the air filters?

It's a shock to find myself here in the middle. I'm pretty much at the halfway point of my life. What on earth? In true muffin-top character, it is not glamorous. This middle is mostly the part where it's easy to pass by without slowing down long enough to pay attention. You just want to tuck that chubby midsection into your pants, drape a flowy shirt over it, and call it "good enough." You know what I'm talking about, yes? What this middle, muffin-top stage of life looks like?

Maybe like me you've now lived longer with your man than without, and that's insane. Because when you were eighteen, maybe you also swore you'd never be anyone's wife or mother, and now he knows every nook, cranny, and (let's face it) pockmark of your "wonderland." And you are a reluctant connoisseur when it comes to the entire range of his nightly snore repertoire. You both wear glasses and secretly enjoy going to Costco. Your kids are toddling into middle school or high school instead of just around your living room. And while on the outside you look like a grown-up, your inside self is still frozen in time at your favorite age, but you no longer recognize the tween celebrities featured on magazines at the checkout aisle.

Instead, you leaf through the home decor mags while waiting to pay for the mound of food it now takes to feed your constantly starving tiny humans who are no longer tiny and sometimes walk into the living room, wink, and call you "Woman!" Your kids are human Shazams for all the songs you no longer recognize on the radio, and when you watch movies these days, you're rooting for the parents instead of the angsty teens.

There are so many soccer and football and dance practices that you often drive to the wrong location or show up at the wrong time on the wrong day. And maybe there's still one little left in the house who gets schlepped along to all the bigs' sporting events, and you end up feeling bad for her and sometimes for yourself that you both have to be on the bleachers so much. None of these are bad things—they're just the pebble stuck in the bottom of your shoe that at first is only annoying but on the hard days makes you want to throw that shoe across the room.

Welcome to the middle!

Normal feels all stretched out and squidgy around the edges when you're splitting time and to-dos, yet it's the stuff of life and marriage and kids and work that everyone lives. And now there's also the reality of retirement as more than just that infomercial you used to fast-forward through but also something you will actually need in the no-longer-distant future. And there's the no-less-essential investment of fighting for time to keep dating the man you're raising kids with so you feel like a couple and not just a couple of people running a summer camp together.

Add to that the more mundane (but still significant) figuring out of new school systems that require you to give five days' advance notice to make a change to the bus schedule and how that complicates organizing playdates for while you're out of town. (Although your kids tell you that you're embarrassing them and "It's not a playdate, Mom; it's called hanging out.") But you're the grown-up, and while this still surprises you, this is the work of grown-ups: organizing the boring details that keep a family chugging along.

This is the stuff of our seasons right now. How we wake up to morning breath and steal quickie Sunday afternoon love and hope we can also squeeze in a just-as-sexy nap. These are the years of driving the curving bends of our neighborhood between school and practices and parent-teacher conferences and games and study sessions and recitals and the gas station and the grocery store, every morning and afternoon and evening and never getting tired of the golden, glorious trees while we often get tired of the driving.

This is just what we do. We drive and feed and keep breaking our days and our lives wide open. We have winding conversations about sports and pop culture and try to explain Kim Kardashian to our tweens while our middles get squishier. It takes work to keep paying attention, to keep parenting with intention, because there's a lazy side of us that just wants to hit cruise control and sleep in now that our kids are sleeping through the night. Please tell me you know what I'm talking about here?

But the stakes are higher now because our kids can remember our mistakes. Combine that with the side of insanity that comes with finally understanding what work you feel meant and fulfilled to do, while also constantly having to juggle it with the schedules of everyone else who lives in your house, including the pets. I've been giving eye drops six times a day to one of my kids and also one of my cats. What on earth? At night the fish need to be fed, and I never remember to actually go pick the tomatoes we tried to grow in our garden this year.

Over and over and over again.

The middle is the place where our lives really live. This is the place where we have grown into the shapes of our souls even as we might have outgrown the shapes of our jeans.

The middle is the marrow. The glorious ordinary of your life that utterly exhausts you but that you might have finally started to understand in ways you didn't at the beginning. Listen, I'm not asking you to *seize* the day here; I'm just asking you to actually *see* it. Even if just out of the corner of one eye. The middle is worth remembering while you are actually living it, because you won't pass by this way again.

So it's worth slowing down long enough on random afternoons to really look around at your life and your husband and the human beings you are raising together and let it sink in that you've grown up and that it's good. You are living at the very center of what will be your story. Right now. Let's stop long enough to read a few lines of these lives out loud. Because trust me when I tell you, sister, the middle is worth reading.

The middle is ridiculous and terrible, so funny and so much fun, and also so exhausting. But it's the stuff of the stories our kids will one day tell about us. These are the days of miracle and wonder. The stories we will one day tell each other as we laugh at all those times we spent all those hours carpooling kids all over the planet of our neighborhood. These are the stories that will line our empty nests one day. We are living the memories that will be passed down to the ones who are still living their beginnings. The middle is the gift you didn't know you were right in the middle of, friend.

Seriously.

Let's relish the middle. Let's savor the middle. Let's embrace the middle in all its mundane glory. Because maybe the middle isn't so bad. Maybe we don't want to hide it, ignore it, or miss it. Sister, maybe the middle is the part where it really starts to get good!

Part 1

Why the Middle of Your Muffin Top Matters

Your Age Is Not a Dirty Word

*O*nce upon a time, I bought a pair of jeans in Prague and they were gorgeous. It was the year before I became a mother. I bought them in a store that was just a stone's throw from the Charles Bridge, and they fit in ways that made Pete and me feel like newlyweds on honeymoon all over again—but better, as we were five years into our marriage and so much better acquainted with each other's moods and bodies than when we were still fumbling our way forward that first year.

Those jeans could tell stories of late nights in expat restaurants ordering onion rings in a country where that phrase is foreign and it would never have occurred to me to consider the calories. Of an afternoon watching *Cats*, an evening at the opera when I briefly ditched the jeans for dressing up, a long walk along the skyline. Those jeans. Those jeans could tell stories on me. And more and more they tell the story of what it means to say goodbye to that shape and that version of myself. Not because there's a perfect size; there's just an irreversible change in the set of the hips, the heart, the fit post-college, post-twenties, post-newlywed, post–new mom, post-thirties and forties, and that's okay. I'm mostly okay with it.

In the mornings now, there are kids clamoring for breakfast, and my eyes are blurry without contacts as I dig into my closet for comfort and bring out a pair of dark-blue denim that is a friendly fit. And my youngest walks over and rubs her cheek against one leg. A teen boy wants cake for breakfast. And I'm more likely wearing my Converse sneakers than my heels.

But my waist can tell stories now bigger and grander than the view from the Charles Bridge in Prague.

I am a life maker, grower of tiny humans, raiser of sons and daughter. I fit into myself better than I ever fit into my Prague jeans. I fit into this house and this family and this story we're living of less newbie parents who still find they enjoy waking up beside kids who some nights have still pretzeled themselves in between us even though they really are too big for that now.

My years made this moment possible. Every single year with all its wild joys and desperate despairs. People are often surprised when I comfortably admit how old I am. And I'm surprised at their surprise. Since when is sharing our age an act of courage? Every single one of these forty-four years has been hard earned. I am proud of them. The older I get, the more I like this woman in this skin. With these hips and these tired eyes and crooked smile and stretch marks and wisdom.

Yes, I'm older.

My middle child thinks it's incomprehensible that I'm in my forties. He likes to ask me over and over again and then shake his head in awe, muttering under his breath, "I thought you were only thirty! Wow, forties!" But I find I fit into this woman's skin better than I did a year ago, and so much better than a decade ago. I am becoming the surest version of myself. I feel it in my heart. Sometimes I feel it in my tired feet, too. But those simply tell me I've been busy. Busy with work and sometimes jogging, more often hauling groceries between the car and the house and carpooling children and walking the length of soccer fields or football fields or the streets of DC with throngs of commuters or relatives in town who want to see the sites, and it is a soulful kind of busy.

I am not afraid anymore of who I will grow up to be—dressed up on Sunday mornings or wound down on Friday nights. I feel the wrinkles climbing happy around my eyes and my cheeks, a testimony to laughter and life. I feel so full of the wonder of being alive. Even on the days I am tired or frustrated or desperate for an hour to myself. I am aware that the God who made me gave me purpose and loves me, not because of what I do, what I weigh, or how I look, but because of who I am, and this is a miracle to me.

My Father God was there during the years of sleep deprivation, and He's still here walking beside me as I keep stubbing my toes on this new season of teenage years. This shift from carrying my kids on the curve of my hip to carrying them deep in the ache of my heart. These strange new years of discovering a fascinating new world that I've arrived in without the instructions or tools I'll need to make sense of it. The tools I'll need to coax my huge boys into sharing their thoughts and dreams with me the way they used to share their Lego creations. This is new. This is good. This is crazy intimidating.

Pete and I are stumbling our way forward and becoming surer in our dreams and work and still get the urge to dash out at 8:30 p.m., after taking the long commute home, to go buy cinnamon breadsticks. It's not just indulgence. Sometimes after a long day of negotiating project deadlines and tween arguments, it's a matter of survival.

This is older. This is better. This is good.

And I know I've made my peace with this time and place when I put on my jeans and care more about their comfort than their size.

These jeans have been on a journey with me and have seen the rise and fall of hips and belly as I carried three babies. I doubt men have closets full of clothes in such a unique array of sizes. But they haven't worn their children on the inside either.

My mom was two years younger than I am now when she died. I remember thinking she was so old. But now, of course, I know better. She was as young as everybody said she was. She had so much living still to do. But she was also satisfied—a woman who ate her life in enthusiastic chunks of joy and roars of laughter and long conversations over many cups of hot tea until she was full up on a full life filled with stories. So I will never be embarrassed by my years.

If I can offer anything I've learned, any mistakes, any scars, any wrinkles of wisdom to the women coming behind me, I will do so. And if letting them know exactly how old I am helps them hear me better, believe me better, or take any of my own experiences to heart, then it was worth it. It is always worth it to be the truest version of ourselves. *Because* of our ages, our sizes, our shapes, our stories.

At night I sit in the bathroom on the closed toilet lid as my youngest, my first grader, takes a bath. And I talk to her about beauty. I point out the parts of her pruney self that she's the most self-conscious about, and we name them beautiful. We talk about round growing bellies that remind us of acorns, packed with all the potential to grow into giant oak trees. This is beauty, I tell her. This belly of yours loves you because it offers you life and length and growth and height, all stored up in there waiting for the right season. She reaches up from the tub and wraps her arms around my neck and we sit there beside the floating dolls that bear witness to this truth, and it's quiet except for the dripping tap.

There are books and blog posts and news articles that I comb through in the dark hours while my daughter sleeps. They say that girls need to hear that they are brave and strong and capable. That their bodies are purposeful more than they are beautiful.

I don't doubt that's true.

But my daughter is fast asleep in the room next door, wrapped around by the pink and white and wildly frilly tutu she wouldn't take off before bed.

And I imagine there's something to that, too.

And last year when we were packing up suitcases for our flight to South Africa and Christmas with the family we hadn't seen in two years, I threw in six princess dresses at the last minute. They were folded up so small and light and fragile into the nooks and crannies of space between our everyday essentials that you'd hardly notice them.

On impulse, I packed a blue Cinderella and a yellow Belle and a white Barbie princess gown. A seafoam-green Ariel dress and a Snow White gown and a bright pink tutu. Part of my brain thought it ridiculous. But I had this other feeling that there may be princesses in need of dresses. The thing about beauty is that it's always there; it just looks different for each of us. But it's always there, waiting to be called out. A grown-up friend wrote me, "I want to be told that I'm beautiful, too."

Behind our glasses and insecurities, behind our unruly bangs and business suits or yoga pants, behind our accomplishments and husbands and kids, there is always the little girl who wants to be told she's beautiful.

I know this because I see her in the mirror.

I ignored her for years. But I'm learning she needs to be taken seriously. Having a daughter is teaching me that. As seriously as I take her brain and her athleticism and her kindness. As seriously as I take her passions and ideas and hurts, I need to take this part of us that is called beauty. Even though I've spent years pretending she doesn't exist. This part of me that embarrasses me, the part that wants nothing to do with Barbies and defines herself by her brain and not her looks. This part of me that longs to be named beautiful.

Because I remember all the ways I did not and was not when I was a young girl. Or when I was a speaker at a conference last week.

She has thin, straggly hair. Her ears stick out.

These are labels I have accepted about myself since I was a teenager because a too-hip-for-his-age hairdresser once whispered them to my mom while he was cutting my hair. As if they were a shameful secret. As if I should apologize for ears that got in the way of his scissors. Do you know what I mean? Do you have a memory, a throwaway sentence, an insult, a note, a casual, cutting observation that you tucked into your soul and allowed to grow up alongside you as if it were always part of you? So that now that lie is grafted into your DNA and you can't tell the difference between the label and the reality of you?

I remember how my cheeks burned. How for years afterward I felt embarrassed anytime a hairdresser came to be trimming in the vicinity. How I imagined they must be appalled by my big and sticky-out ears. How that tiny seed of an insult had grown into a definition that I allowed to define me. How easily I slipped into the habit of apologizing for my appearance even if I spoke the defeated words only inside my own head.

He named me unbeautiful, and I believed him.

I wonder what would have happened if my mother had voiced a response to the sentence that slipped so carelessly from that hairdresser all those years ago. I wonder, with all of life's long lists of busyness, if moments like those even qualify for taking the time to respond. For leaning in and telling strangers who casually pin unhelpful words to parts of our bodies that we will, in fact, not be accepting those labels today, thank you very much. That we choose instead to name our girls and ourselves—and, yes, even our thighs and ears and waists and hair and scars—with the words spoken on the sixth day of creation, "*very good*" (Genesis 1:31).

And then one afternoon, decades later in South Africa, the women in our family have a princess party for our daughters—some adopted, some fostered, some born from our hips—and I see in each of their wide eyes and longing looks at the mirror that beauty loves to be called out, to be named and cherished and recognized by her mother.

Our daughters will see themselves as beautiful in our eyes first. If we let them. And once they've seen themselves as beautiful in the eyes of their mothers, maybe they'll be braver dancing through the minefields of what the movies and magazines scream is desirable.

On a whim, the moms dress up too. The only princess dresses that fit us are the ones from our weddings. I haven't worn mine since that day, and it won't zip up all the way in the back. But I step into it anyway and see my own wild hopes echoed in five pairs of eyes. I see that beauty is more than a dress size and, at the same time, never less than princess size. I see that God looks at our insides but also made our unique outsides and that maybe we need to stop making false divides.

And I feel how I am wired to feel beautiful as five sets of small arms wrap tightly around my neck, and I believe the promise that the future holds love stories for each of us.

Daughters lost and found, abandoned, beloved, adopted.

Daughters named.

Daughters in all different shades, accents, languages.

Daughters celebrated.

Daughters *beautiful.*

And the word might not always fit us. It might feel as if it's too tight or stuck in back like my wedding dress that gaped open with a disgruntled zipper that couldn't quite contain the twenty years since I last wore it. But it doesn't matter. It doesn't matter that I've outgrown that dress, because you can't ever outgrow the beauty of being loved.

And when my mini-me, my little girl, takes my veil and wraps it around herself like a hug, eyes looking up at me from under layers of lace, I see my past, present, and future all cupped in that single moment in the hands of the God who declares us all beautiful: "He has made *everything* beautiful in its time" (Ecclesiastes 3:11).

That means you and me and our years, our hurts and unhappy endings. Everything is beautiful when reflected in the eyes of the God who names us so. Beauty—like so much grace, so much hope, so many promises—is in the eye of the faithful, heavenly beholder. But it's okay to doubt. It's okay to wonder. It's okay to ask the question out loud, sister. Even if the only person who hears it is the one who made you beautiful in the first place. But, hear me; hear *Him* when He says that you *are* beloved and wildly beautiful.

From your cracked, tired heels to your fingers all wrinkled from dishwater and diapers changed in the dark. From your brain bursting with curiosity and creativity and entrepreneurship and equations to your hair that you wish was curlier, straighter, thicker, thinner.

That mole, that wrinkle, those jeans that don't fit like they used to on that set of hips. Those tired eyes, those strong arms, that crooked grin, that brilliant mind.

That brave mouth that speaks up for children, for women, for anyone who can't speak for themselves. Those feet that run hard after a God who has called you.

Those aching muscles, that broken heart, that doubting faith.

Every freckle.

Every laugh line.

Every stretch mark.

Every wrinkle.

Every year.

That waist that deserves your grace.

Yes, even that belly, all soft with the memory of life.

Especially that.

Every inside *and* every outside.

You. Are. Beautiful.

The Scale Is Not the Boss of You

*M*y dad was turning seventy, so our family was making the trek to South Africa from Baltimore to Johannesburg via Detroit and Amsterdam. To be back with my people. The people who were my first home.

We were ordering gifts and getting new suitcases and planning all the family we wanted to see. But deep down I was wasting my anticipation because I was drowning in self-conscious worry. Worry I wished I could turn off like the dripping faucet it was.

Here's the thing—just one summer earlier I was at the healthiest, fittest weight I'd been in years. Then I faced some crushing work deadlines and mainlined candy corn, cotton candy, carbs, and other assorted forms of sugar to push myself through.

There are things a forty-plus-year-old body does not recover from quickly. Or even slowly. Heavy, sustained sugar and carb intake combined with zero exercise is one of them. No matter that I panic-joined a gym and actually went several times a week. No matter that I cut out the late-night binging on French bread and Brie cheese.

Let's just pause here to take a moment to celebrate the gift that is Brie cheese.

One of my favorite food memories of all time involved Brie cheese and Kyiv, Ukraine. A friend and I discovered a fancy, hoity-toity deli one afternoon in downtown Kyiv and lost our minds when we saw the bread and cheese selection. We bought it by the basketful. And because we couldn't restrain ourselves and suffer the commute home before we dug in, we stood on the sidewalk at a busy intersection waiting for a taxi while shoving huge chunks of warm bread covered in ripped-off gobs of gooey cheese into our eager mouths. And washing it all down with Coke straight from the bottle. That street corner and that Brie baguette sandwich in the spring sunshine were pure culinary heaven.

Flash-forward to present time. Because I'd spent months reliving those memories at a much more advanced age—no matter that I was really, really trying—the scale was still depressingly stubborn every morning I stepped onto it. And I felt my heart sink with every pound I hadn't lost yet. My days filled up with self-beratement about my lack of discipline and why couldn't I survive on less calories and why do I love food so much?

You see, I'm a joy eater. The happier I am, the more I want to indulge. Food feels like happiness to me. It's like a hug from the inside. Give me family anxiety or rocky relationships or hard conversations or kid drama and I lose all appetite. But give me new friends or coffee dates or a house full of guests and I will break out the dips and chips and well-loved Crock-Pot and Joanna Gaines's banana bread and delight the night away.

Better yet, combine my two favorite things—a dear friend and her kitchen—and I will bliss out entirely. Serve me up heartfelt conversation alongside homemade biscuits and I could easily kill a decade of time like that.

I sat in Wendy's tiny kitchen in Kyiv as she coaxed kefir into buttermilk so she could make southern biscuits from scratch in a country that didn't sell them. Her oven warmed the room, the conversation warmed my soul, and the biscuits filled up all the empty places that homesickness had eaten away.

I sat in Christie's farmhouse kitchen in Pennsylvania and she shrugged and told me lunch wouldn't be much and then cut into crusty French baguettes and tossed Greek salad with its shiny black olives and tart onions with her homemade vinaigrette and I sat on her kitchen stool for hours feeding my belly and my heart.

My mother was a terrible cook but a gifted curator of conversations, people, and comfort food. These are my happy places. So when I'm happy I go there. Over and over. Without discipline or restraint. And in my forties I have discovered that that kind of happiness takes a toll on my middle. Well, on my middle, my thighs, and my double chin, too, apparently.

So while the kitchen was my confidant, the scale became an angry voice in my head. A voice that despised my thighs and my belly and spoke ruthless criticism at both. And I listened. And tried really hard to obey.

And it sucked the life and marrow out of this long-anticipated trip home.

Then one Thursday I woke up and decided I was tired of it.

I got on the phone with my dad and fessed up. I told him just how tired I was of feeling tired of worrying about my weight. I said, "Well, Dad, we're coming home chubbier than we would have liked, and we're hoping you guys will just take us as we are."

My dad. My dad who was turning seventy and is a fantastically health-conscious doctor and runs five miles a couple of times a week and is raising adopted kids the same age as mine while still consulting hundreds of patients a week and who probably never binge-ate anything in his life.

My dad.

But the guilt and judgment never came.

Instead, I could feel the love unfurling across the miles of phone lines and into my ear as he said, "We'll love you just the way you are. And we hope when you're home, you'll let us add on a few more pounds for good measure, of all the foods here that we know you miss!"

I was so surprised, a belly laugh bubbled up out of me. I was surprised by the joy that so easily eclipsed the worry and burst out into laughter. I cradled the phone against my ear and it was like being home already.

Listen, this isn't about food or weight. Well, it is in the sense that healthy matters and great company is just as great with way less carbs. That's all true. And moving our bodies matters because they thrive with exercise and it gets every part of us firing on all cylinders. I get that. I hear you preaching the importance of healthy food and consistent exercise—I really truly do—and I will keep at it.

But it's also about much more than that. Really. It's about that old love story. It's about believing that you are unconditionally loved. No, it's more than that. It's about *knowing* that you are unconditionally loved no matter what you look like, weigh in at, sound like, talk like, think like.

Do you know what that means? Beyond the cliché that we are so good at brushing off? Let me spell it out for you the way I had to spell it out for myself:

Unconditional love = you are loved, no matter what.

No matter what the scale says or your performance review says or your passive-aggressive relationship says or your bathing suit says or the voice in your head says.

You are loved beyond pounds or fit or style or perfection.

You are loved because *you are*.

Period. End of story.

You are loved because you were created by a God who *is* love.

You are loved because love is the DNA of the stuff you were made from.

You are loved because love is the blood that runs in your veins and the sway of your hips and, yes, even the rub of your upper thighs against each other—love, love, love, left, right, left, right, swish, swish, love, love, love. Even in the sticky sweat of summer in places you wish weren't sweating.

You are loved because love is what pumps in your veins like a drumbeat reminder that this is your name and there is no other name than love, love, love.

Somehow between the scale and my favorite jeans that don't fit this summer, I forgot that. My daughter was stroking my belly this morning and whispered into its curves, "I love this belly." And my dad said the same thing using different words on the phone this morning. And my husband said it when he called to say he missed me while he's traveling this week.

This throbbing harmony of how loved we are. If only we would listen. If only we would stop listening to our measuring sticks and scales, these voices that we need to quit, and start listening to our promises. For God Himself says, "I will never leave you or abandon you" (Hebrews 13:5, csb).

Don't get me wrong—I will continue on this journey to be healthy for my kids and for the calling God has entrusted to me. I will practice curbing my sugar cravings and leaning into better choices in my fridge and in my heart. I will keep moving my body and reminding my muscles that they are made for more than sitting behind a computer all day.

But at the same time, I will leave behind the voices that are robbing me of the joy of that journey. Don't ever let the scale tell you different.

And I will practice being loved, more than I practice being careful what I eat.

And next week I will fly home to my South African people and revel in rusks and pancakes and boerewors and pap and koeksisters and a whole host of foods that taste like home. And I will not consult the scale for its opinion.

I will look into the eyes of my family and let them have the last word, because I already know what my Father says: "I have loved you with an everlasting love; I have drawn you with unfailing kindness" (Jeremiah 31:3).

And before I step onto a scale, I will repeat those words out loud and let them, and only them, be the weight that defines me.

My Favorite Muffin-Top Photo

I was one of the oldest kindergarten moms our third (and final) lap around, as we started this whole parenthood thing much later than most folks. So while other moms were vying for one of the field-trip-chaperone spots, I was deeply relieved to be able to sit it out. Over the past decade, I have seen so many field trips that I've lost any sense of wonder. Also, I get violently carsick. Riding a sticky school bus crammed full of overexcited six-year-olds is a special level of motion-sickness hell. So this mama has learned that if you have to do field-trip duty, you want it to be from your minivan while following behind the school bus, drinking your Starbucks and listening to your favorite podcast.

But kindergarten end-of-year plays are another thing entirely. Give them *all* to me. Bring them on, I say. They are magic and fairy dust and hopes and dreams, and they (almost) make up for the endless hours spent signing reading folders and slogging through sight words.

This end-of-year performance is what schools use to erase all the nightmares of trying to come up with a hundred different items to glue to your kid's shirt to commemorate the first one hundred days of school. (On that note, you really should be shooting for only minimal output and expense. Just ask any seasoned mom. So just say no to tiny, messy sequins and yes to soft, easy-to-handle mini pom-poms. Or better yet, just stick with plain-old stickers.)

I've also learned that if you want a good seat for the kindergarten play, you need to arrive a good forty minutes early because kindergarten parents and all their camera paraphernalia take this thing very seriously. So you better be early or forget even seeing your kid because you'll be crowded out by rows and rows of video equipment and selfie sticks.

Zoe's first (and our last) kindergarten performance was epic. Yes, I can say that with a straight face. Because you put a roomful of generally sane adults in front of row upon row of their offspring spouting off incomplete and garbled sentences, combined with an awkward musical soundtrack and nonsensical hand motions, and we will just eat it all up 100 percent. It's biology at its most basic.

So there we were feeling as if our daughter had won an acting scholarship to Juilliard because she had a "speaking role" as the brickhouse pig. True story. Although, perhaps these overexaggerated feelings were more mine than Peter's, but whatever, man. My kid was in the cutest Peppa Pig T shirt and tutu, and I was *all in* for her one line yelled loudly and proudly into the microphone.

I cried. Yes. I did. Go on, admit that you cry too when your tiny humans go through the brave motions of putting themselves out there. It's irresistible. This glimpse into what's waiting for them out there in the big, wide world. It's like getting to watch them put a toe in the water. Vulnerability and courage are both required. And our miniature adults troop right up there in front of a giant audience of expectations and cameras, and it's impossible to be disappointed by them. We're too busy being in awe of them.

So she said her line and sang her songs and we clapped and cheered from the front row. We leaned in and watched it all with our own eyes, carefully not overdoing the camerawork so our girl could get a glimpse of our faces, unobscured by screens. We watched and laughed and loved that moment of being swept up in the sea of other people all feeling similar emotions. All that pride heavy in the air, and all those parents and grandmas and grandpas, aunties and uncles, all clapping their hands raw and holding on to these memories to save up in their heads for the days their kindergarteners grow up and away from them and these tender moments when they were still those kids' everything.

Peter brought Zoe a bouquet of flowers. Third child, first daughter. What can I say? We're fools for her. And she swept it up in her arms as her daddy swept her up in his, and her smile was sunshine and we grinned back, defenseless against her gravitational pull. I absorbed it all through my eyes and my skin and then decided to take a picture so I could save it up for the days I needed to see it all over again.

We navigated our way up onto the stage between all the other families, and she wanted to pose in front of her brick house. So we squeezed ourselves into an open spot on the set and then she reached for me and I wrapped my arm around those precious shoulders and she held her flowers high and we both turned full-wattage smiles on the camera. What a moment. What a daughter. God bless you, kindergarten teachers all over the world, for making magic in tired school gyms!

Peter snapped the photo, and Zoe and I laughed our way off the stage and out to lunch—she wanted a Happy Meal from McDonald's—and only later at home did I pull up that photo. And the first time I opened it, all I saw was radiant joy. But the second look brought a different perspective. I was taken aback to see my own stomach in such a prominent view. I had crouched down on the stage next to my tiny daughter without wasting a second on rearranging my limbs or the drape of my shirt or sucking in my gut. I was much too focused on her. And it distracted me utterly from myself. So what you see in the photo is a beaming mother with a generous muffin top bulging over her jeans as she presses up next to her daughter.

I looked at the photo with what should have been dismay. But I can tell you honestly, my finger was never even tempted to hit the trash button. No way. There was too much happiness to ever diminish it by worrying about waistlines. Sometimes the joy of our kids drowns out the insecurities about ourselves, and dang, that's such a good thing. It's rare and it happened to me in that moment. I wasn't thinking about posing in the most flattering position because I was so busy exploding with delight and pride and love in my girl.

I looked at that photo and all I could see was how bright she shines. How joy bursts out of her face and explodes all over her mama. When I look at her I forget to worry about me, my hair, my pose, my outfit, my body image. All I see is her and she is the whole world, and, dear Jesus, please help me keep focusing less on me and more on her and let that spill over into other parts of my life too.

Help me to keep forgetting myself in the healthiest kinds of ways. And keep seeing the world through the sparkling, wild, and wonderful eyes of someone else! Because when she looks at herself—and, even more, when she looks at me—all she sees is admiration, a best friend, the excitement of all she has to look forward to in becoming a woman. The deep celebration of who she is and how she accepts this all as her due.

It's made me wonder. It's made me try to find the line in time. The point between then and now that explains the how. How we women can go from the childlike delight in who we are—laughing, loving, running with abandon on unselfconscious legs—to running for the work of losing those last few pounds. And then some more after that. You know what I mean, right, sister?

It makes me want to find the location on the map, the longitude and latitude that mark the spot where the mirror became a critic instead of simply a reflection of all that beauty that rises from the inside with the tide of a life well loved.

Who taught us to hate the shape of a gentle belly still softly swollen with the memory of life? Or those flabbier-than-we-might-like arms that soothe and rock and circle the years of tiny lives who take comfort in that softness, who find a pillow there for hot, tired tears.

Who drew the line between before and after this body bore kids or walked the long road of adoption or of in vitro fertilization and felt in every nerve ending all the changing and stretching and aching of the metamorphosis of motherhood? Who said that stretch of growth wouldn't ring us around with age?

Who taught us to be ashamed, sister?

Who stole the glory of motherhood by measuring it in pounds or wrinkles or saggy arms instead of lives, first breaths and steps, and heartbreaking conversations? In gotcha days and late nights waiting up, in misunderstandings and forgiveness and the weight of immeasurable, shockingly ordinary glory?

Look at the oak and her honorable life marked down to the very bones of her body. Each year of growth and change and breaking and reaching still higher for the heavens marked with ring upon ring of hard, beautiful life that she doesn't try to hide.

When did disguise become as necessary to being a mother as having children?

Instead, the oak trees bend and sing in the wind, their rings recognizing layer upon layer of life. Lean in, sister, because this is our story, too.

It's time to own our years. It's time to own each year and baby and change as beautiful as the body of the tall, wild, wonderful oak so comfortable in her skin. So I trace the memories engraved into the laugh lines of my face, the dimples in my belly, the wrinkles that wink from the corners of my eyes.

My reminder sits next to me. "You're so beautiful, Mama," she says. And I know she means it. She tells me the exact same thing every morning—when I'm fresh out of the shower with a sometimes-successfully outlined eye and jeans that aren't sagging yet—as she does at night when we're both exhausted and the mascara has smudged dark circles beneath my eyes.

Her skin is as flawless as her innocence. And I don't want to be the first to paint over it. Not with the baggage handed down from one woman to the next—the secret sigh of the scale—that whispers malcontent over a lifetime of meals.

I get that healthy matters. It's just that I want her soul to grow up well fed.

So I let her fingers trace patterns on the tummy that stretched to house her baby body. I don't erase it from the photo. I share the moment on Instagram and print it for our family album. Zoe and me and my muffin top.

We sit side by side on the bed, and I show her the photo from her concert and she admires us both. We talk about her courage, her favorite parts from the play, her outfit, and then talk slips to our summer plans and how we both have strong legs. She softly traces the scars that punctuate mine. And I tell her the stories behind them.

She sees me laugh into the mirror and watches my reflection in her father's eyes—how he makes me beautiful because it's how he sees me.

"We're girls," I whisper into her curls, and she giggles and hugs me hard, all arms and legs wrapped tight around the body I practice loving.

I practice. Deliberately loving every season of this body that has been gifted to me. Standing with arms spread wide against the rising tide of dissatisfaction our culture shouts about women. She whispers back to me as we're crouched down on the edge of a stage—me and my muffin top and joy and she in her self-confidence and joy—"Mama, you my vewy, vewy, vewy best friend."

And I am determined to be just that in words and actions and the love story that, ring after ring, I live in this body.

The Love Story of Turning Forty

*T*oday it's in the high eighties and the last thing that makes sense is to put on leggings and head to the gym. But I do. I roll out in the old white minivan, windows down, and let the music and the kid-free quiet settle into the hot seats along with my legs, which haven't run anywhere in way too long.

My exercise goals aren't big. I'm not shooting for a *Vogue* or *Cosmo* size. I go to the gym for company and a place to fling back these shoulders that have spent too long hunched over a keyboard. The music is already thumping through the floorboards when I arrive. Funny how joy can sound like a Latin beat and a roomful of women all stomping in time.

I'm not the oldest or the youngest in the room. No one knows my name. But I feel so deeply welcome. All that's required is a willingness to sweat. I do. I feel it running down my back, and it heals me in places that have been asleep for too long. I need to move like this. I know it will hurt tomorrow, but right now I need this room and these women. They remind me of all that is good and beautiful and strong with my gender.

There are several old enough to be my mom. In all shades of

human. Dancing, dancing with flair and all the rhythm that I seem to have lost. Their hips sing and I grin and try not to catch my own eye in the mirror, because I know I'll just laugh at my off-balance reflection.

But these women with sinews and thighs and strong hands are too busy celebrating this business of being alive. This love song to humanity. It's impossible to look away.

Did you know that Jesus showed up in a gym in Northern Virginia yesterday? He looked a lot like His daughters.

All this determination they have to put His creation through the motions. To feel the blood pump and thump and the smiles crack at the end of a routine. These women, all exhausted and exhilarated and connected by a class that happens every week, wildly reflecting His strength and beauty.

I keep at it. Even though the clock hand moves so slowly and the class feels like forever, I stop counting minutes and start counting women. Long hair stuck down her back. Short legs over there. Strong arms next to me, and the accountant one row away who moves like a dancer in her own spotlight.

I love them so much, these women I don't know. I love them.

So strong, so capable, so beloved.

I would write them a love song if I could—the sisterhood of bold hearts who throw themselves into unselfconscious Zumba and who don't know how brave they are until they do.

Until they get up at 4:30 a.m. to provide for those kids. Until they are cut and bleed to deliver that baby. Until they serve in the homeroom year in and year out. Until they meet the ambulance at the hospital. Until they say goodbye to their parents, their homes, their jobs, the version of themselves they've known best for decades. Until they rearrange beds to make room for foster kids, new neighbors, space to host community groups in their basements.

So much brave beating in time to a hallelujah chorus on the sound system.

So much remarkable.

So much strength.

And on the days I remember to pay attention, I see how we're all still wild with the wonder of being women.

I drive home and the sweat tastes good on my upper lip. I take out crisp lettuce and plump cherry tomatoes for lunch. I slowly cut up a pear to slice on top of it all and grab the homemade vinaigrette waiting in the fridge. I sit down at the table and look out the window and I'm forty.

I got my first mammogram yesterday.

It felt brave and beautiful to take care of me. Of this one mom and one wife in this family.

And it felt especially beautiful to be required not to wear lotions, because that meant I went ahead and left off my makeup, too. I'm forty and this is my unfiltered skin, and I love it more now than I did when I was eighteen. Probably because I'm so much more comfortable in it.

And I don't take it quite as much for granted now as I did then.

My friends ask me what I want for my birthday. A tea party, I tell them. They laugh and say they don't drink tea; they prefer coffee. "Tea it is!" I say. No presents, just the gifts of themselves.

So they each bring their favorite kind of tea-party food and the gift of words. This is what I want to feast on: the company of friends and the words they decide to speak over me as I enter this fifth decade of my life.

Lisa, Rose, Christy, Karine, Christie, and me. We sit down to a tea party and it's beautiful. Late August sings with sunshine that doesn't bake but rather warms your bones. We sit around the tiny dining room table Peter and I have had since we got married, and each place is set with the teacups and saucers that were wedding gifts, wildflowers in old jam jars, and paper napkins. It's the perfect kind of non-fancy fancy and I string up the "Tea Time" banner that Karine made out of book pages across the window.

I am not a good cook, but I throw a phenomenal tea party. Chalk it up to my English/South African roots, but I know about the charm of teapots and cold milk and lumps of sugar. About flower buds and cucumber sandwiches and melktert made just like all the aunties back home in South Africa make for every church bake sale. Rose has brought blueberry soufflés baked in delicate blue ramekins and we pour sweet lemonade into wine glasses.

Never underestimate the power of a tea party to transport you out of time and into a place where there is no rush, where there is lingering conversation and finger foods. There is space to hear and be heard, and there is going to be a warm spot under your rib cage, right where the tea hits home.

We linger. We refill the teapots. And each of my friends offers the gift of words. Some share specifics; some speak promises for the future; some pray. I sit with my hands wrapped around my teacup and soak in their generosity. I soak in their friendship. I eat their words until my stomach and heart can almost not take in another bite. I am forty and I am finally home. Here in this rental house surrounded by these women who know how to welcome me in.

Forty, I discover, is a new beginning, and my friends hold the door wide open for me. A welcome arrival into a time when we get to choose more of what we love and less of what we used to think mattered. More friendship, less comparison. More generosity, less competition. More slow, less rush. More savor, less striving. More gathering, less hosting. More casual, less stressed. I see all of this sitting around my table in the eyes of these wise women who welcome me into forty with their words, their laughter, their time.

Lean in, sister, because here is the part of the story where you can choose to celebrate your body instead of constantly despising it. Where all your scars and stretch marks stand for something and all the women ahead of you stand up to cheer you on. Where you can make room at the table for your sisters coming up behind you, as well as those already further down the road.

Sister, here is the part of the story where you realize we were family all along. Where you know deep down in your bones that we are better together because we are all part of a body infinitely valuable to the God who names each one of us priceless. Where we share all the inside stories about makeup tips and yet feel completely comfortable running errands in our sweatpants. Here is the plot twist where we finally discover that good enough is actually more than enough.

Here is where we finally learn to extend ourselves grace and then to pass huge chunks of it down the line to the women around us. Here is where we drink tea in the middle of an ordinary afternoon and there is nothing ordinary about it at all.

Part 2

Why the Middle of Your Marriage Matters

When You Think Your Love Story Is Boring

My love life will never be satisfactory until someone runs
through an airport to stop me from getting on a flight.
—TEENAGER POST OF THE WEEK, *Huffington Post*

*T*hree times he's held my hands, my shaking legs, my head, my
heart as I've borne down and groaned a baby into being. He
has run for ice chips and doctors and lived night shifts and
lain himself low to help me hold on through the hard rock and roll and
push and pull of labor, and I've never drowned holding on to his hand.

There is a rumor, an urban myth, a fiction, a fantasy, a black-and-
white screen cliché that love looks like the mad, romantic dash through
airports for a last chance at a flailing kiss.

And then the credits roll.

And the lights come on.

And we must go back to our real lives, where we forget that love
really lives.

One night in a farmhouse in Pennsylvania, I threw up so hard and fast and often that I couldn't stand come morning. He moved over and out and gave me the bed. He went out for crackers and soda and played mind-numbing games to keep the three kids occupied and away from Mom.

I looked in the mirror and there was nothing romantic looking back at me, but around the wrinkles in my eyes and the parched white cheeks, there was the deep romance of being loved beyond how I looked.

He's never run through an airport for me.

He's gone out for milk at 10 p.m., and he's held our children through bouts of stomach viruses. He's carried us on his shoulders when we were too tired or too sad or too done to keep doing the every-day ins and outs that make up life.

He's unloaded a hundred loads of laundry and put the dishes away.

He lays down his life, and it looks like so many ordinary moments stitched together into the testimony of a good man who comes home to his family driving the old minivan, the one with the broken air-conditioning.

It undoes me every time to look around and find him there, having my back in the day-to-day and the late night into late night and then next year again.

He's run a thousand times around the sun with me, and we hold hands and touch feet at night between the covers. Even when we're wretched and fighting, we're always fighting our way back to each other.

He's never run through an airport for me.

He runs on snatched sleep and kids tucked into his shoulder on both sides of the bed.

He is patient and kind.

He always protects, always trusts, always hopes, always perseveres.

And we come running to him. When the battered white minivan pulls into the driveway, his children trip over themselves, their abandoned Crocs, and the pool bag to be the first to open the door and spill out their day into the hands of the man who can catch them.

He's never run through an airport for me.

This ordinary, unremarkable love walks slowly alongside every day. One step, one day, one football practice at a time. One permission slip signed, one Lunchable, one school play, one art project, one Lego box, one more nighttime cup of water delivered at a time.

This ordinary love that wakes up with bad breath and crease marks on his cheeks and is the daily bread that sustains across time zones and countries and cultures and the exhaustion of trying to figure out how to be a parent and a grown-up and somebody's forever.

And this is a love life: to live each small, sometimes unbearably tedious moment . . . together. To trip over old jokes and misunderstandings. To catch our runaway tongues and tempers and tenderly trust them to the person who now knows firsthand our better and our much worse.

He lets me warm my ice-cold feet between his legs and the covers at night.

He's never run through an airport for me.

But he goes to Walmart at 9:30 p.m. for back-to-school supplies that we've had all summer to get and of course have left till the last minute. When he walks into the living room at 11:00 p.m. with bags full of the obligatory red, green, yellow, and blue folders and all the million pre-sharpened number-two pencils, it's the sexiest thing I've seen all week.

This is love with the lights on and eyes wide open. This is the brave love, the scared love, the sacred boring, the holy ordinary, over sinks of dirty dishes and that one cupboard in the kitchen with the broken hinge.

That Time I Thought I Lost My Wedding Ring

A few months back, I was sure I'd put my wedding ring on the bedside table. The ring I've had for twenty years. The one we bought in South Africa.

I was sure I'd put the ring on that bedside table, the one with the crackly white primer I'd never actually gotten around to painting with a topcoat. I can see the ring in my mind's eye, right next to the lamp with the crooked hand-me-down shade.

But the next morning, the ring wasn't where I remembered leaving it before turning off the light.

I looked everywhere.

I moved the bed, the table—basically half the room got shoved up against the opposite wall so I could search better and deeper. I found plenty of stray socks and dust and other gross odds and ends that lurk beneath beds. But no ring.

I told myself it wasn't time to worry yet. That once we packed up for our big move, the ring would be unearthed from beneath all the chaotic living we did in that rental.

But on the last day of our lease, on a hot and sweaty June morning when the room was bare naked, there was still no sign of the ring. There was just a small pile of leftover life—dust bunnies, hair ties, and such—crouching in the middle of the floor. I got down on my hands and knees and sifted through it. I was certain the ring still had to exist somewhere inside that room.

But beyond hope, it didn't.

My diamond ring, given to me by my Michigan boy on bended knee along the lakes of the Notre Dame campus, was officially gone.

I could feel my heart tell me that maybe now was, after all, time to be sad.

And then we move and unpack and paint and sit out on the front porch with the new neighbors and learn more about koi fish than I realized there is to know.

And then we fly to Florida for two weeks with my in-laws, and my daughter sleeps on her couch pillow bed right beside us, her soft snuffling snores punctuating the night. And when Pete crawls in next to me, we lie under the fan and unpack the best parts of the day together. He whispers how he likes having her in the room with us. And I agree, because her soft breathing rings us around with reminders of what a gift her life is.

All week our sons keep running between their wonder on the beach and Pete and me to show off their speed and their discoveries. And Zoe is their dedicated shadow, the three of them racing along the shore.

Stretched out in a line that lights up between the horizon and the sunset they run.

They run rings between us.

And I braid Zoe's hair to keep her curls out of the tangly fingers of the sea. I braid her hair in the mornings and unbraid it at night, and her curls ring around my fingers.

There are some things that are true whether we believe them or not.

There are some things that are true whether we have proof of them or not.

There are some things that are true whether we have the movie moments to highlight them or not.

I don't need a tan line on my left ring finger to tell me that.

Pete and I hold hands quietly while our kids shriek in delight, wave after wave of salty joy crashing up to their ankles. We walk in their footsteps, and this is what twenty years of commitment looks like.

The man who carries the buckets and the shovels and the bags stops to photograph his tween son's desperately proud abs.

These moments ring around us, and the ocean stretches out in front, and this is married.

This is our promise that we keep making again and again between the dishes and the bedtime dance and the routine of reminding the boys to each brush for more than twenty seconds. Rings of dirt around the bathtub, and bright-blue toothpaste rings around the sink.

Rings of what feels like never-ending requests for stories or water or "just one more bowl of cereal before bed."

Tight monkey hugs ring around our ribs, and three faces peer over their shoulders to make sure we're still there as they run wild at the world.

We are. Tonight and tomorrow. Between bad dreams and skies on fire with wonder. As I tuck myself between the band of his arms and realize that I never did lose my ring in the first place.

A Time to Fight

I had four minutes before I was supposed to get on a Facebook Live interview, when I screamed at my husband so hard that it hurt my throat. I screamed and a painful week's worth of all the things I hadn't said came crashing out my mouth. All the things I'd kept locked behind closed doors screamed into the room between us as he stared at me from the other side of the bed and I couldn't make it stop.

Neither the ticking clock nor the impending interview nor the makeup that was threatening to run could stop the words pouring out of me. I screamed at the man who gets up while it is still dark and dresses in the living room so as not to wake me. But right then, he wasn't that guy, and we both knew it. We were living through a season of many unsaid frustrations, and when that is true, no matter how quietly you both tiptoe around them, one evening you're going to find that the filter splits at the seams and that all the things you've been holding in become an avalanche you can't hold back. It's especially awkward when the timing is right before you're supposed to lead a live video hangout for your primarily Christian online community.

I remember how when we first got married, books and wiser friends used to tell us things like, "You need to learn to fight fair." I had no idea what that meant. I knew in the literal sense that it meant not to fight dirty with cutting sarcasm or underhanded passive aggression or snow-ball reminders of every other thing the other person has done wrong in the past decade. But I didn't really know that it also meant that fighting will, in fact, be *necessary*. That you will need to find a healthy way to say the hard things that make you angry. You will need to give your anger to someone in a way that helps the individual and you make sense of the storm. A way to navigate it rather than simply ignore it.

Ignorance is not bliss in a marriage. Ignorance is more likely avoidance. And then one day, ignorance is an avalanche.

We'd avoided talking about my frustrations with our current routines and struggles and sense of total isolation when he gets lost in his own head and forgets to include me in the story he's living. But I'm a verbal processor, so the less he talked to me, the more I yelled inside my own head. But I locked up that yelling voice and told it I needed to be supportive and give him space and grant grace because those are all good things. They are.

But it's hard for those good things to take root and grow into a garden of real conversation and connection if you stuff them up in the attic of your mind and use them to paint over the layers of resentment and gritty frustration that are building up in there. That junk will eventually rot right through the floorboards and fall into your lap when you least expect it. For me it was right before a Facebook Live. Like literally four minutes before.

Peter watched me screaming and I watched myself screaming and part of my brain thought, *This is really interesting. Something here needs to come out into the light of day so we can talk about it instead of scream about it.*

Earlier that night, he'd had one of our sons at a sports practice and I'd stayed home to clean up dinner and prep the house and my presentation. I had the other two in bed, so all Pete had to do was walk in the door and go into our bedroom with his laptop and unwind with a good dose of Netflix while I hosted the live event from my own laptop at the dining room table. But because this is real life, my daughter wouldn't stay in her room and wanted to sleep in our room, and somehow this set off a chain reaction because instead of helping get her settled so I could kick things off on the live-show countdown, my husband, my partner, suddenly became obtuse and unhelpful and brought out the side-eye and frustrated sighs. My mama guilt collided with my work stress and ran headlong into my marriage frustration and . . . Chernobyl.

At its core, marriage means having the other person's back. This is hard on good days. But on bad days or bad months when we're all stretched thinner than parchment paper, and the smallest, tiniest word can rip the fragile structure right through the middle, we have to dig extra deep for the guts to choose to have the other guy's back. Especially when we're not sure we've got it in us. Even then we need to lean into our reserves and offer kindness when tiredness is mostly what we've got to work with.

So in that moment when all Pete came up with was a spark of complaint, my own bone-dry tank, filled with only the fumes of leftover resentment and deep emptiness, crackled into an explosion that lit us both on fire.

We've been married twenty years and still manage to utterly misunderstand each other. These are the real-life love stories.

Living alongside another human being, in the same house and bed and bathroom, takes infinite adaptability. A sense of humor also helps.

So does intentional self-awareness. But when you're also living alongside many smaller human beings who are growing up into their own selves and constantly need you to help them navigate the way, sucking your time and energy and often the very nutrients from your bones, this sometimes leaves only scraps of attention, of grace and compassion and passion, for the marriage. This is the danger zone.

Peter and I spend hours reading for our jobs, and because we're both fascinated learners, it turns out we both read a lot of books that provide insight into who we are. But that's no good if we forget to actually share those insights with each other. It doesn't help if he has spent years studying his Enneagram type and mapping and making sense of himself and his behavior if he doesn't also offer that information to me. Turns out he'd been walking around with the key to helping unlock some of our worst misunderstandings but never actually handed it over to me.

I do the same thing.

I am a born and groomed people pleaser who feels physically incapable of relaxing until all her people are safe and served and settled. Not so they have a sense of well-being, not as an act of generosity, but because my insides cannot exhale until I know that no one is going to need anything more from me. I need to be excused—or maybe *released* is a better word—before I feel permission to rest. Until then I feel as though I'm handcuffed to their needs. I can feel trapped until each person communicates some version of "I'm fine. I'm good. Thanks for taking care of me, Mom, but you've got permission to take the rest of the night off."

However, until that moment, until that secret and bizarre signal is sent that only my people-pleasing antennae can pick up on (and that my family doesn't even realize I'm waiting for), I'm running on empty. Little do they know that what from the outside looks like a mom who is cleaning up and washing dishes and serving a last snack as the family enjoys a TV show is really just a mom waiting for a chance to bark at one of those ungrateful brats for keeping her on duty so long.

Yeah, it's kinda insane when I type it out.

But my counselor explained it to me. Yes, I went to see a counselor. Not because of this and not because of the night I screamed at Peter but because of something else. And it turns out that all the pieces were related. I love my counselor. Going to see her is like laying out all these puzzle bits and pieces of my life that I can't make sense of and then her slowly moving them around and showing me the connections until I can start to see the picture emerge. I'd never seen a counselor before. I didn't even know how to find one. I just Googled "Christian counselors near me" and got connected with a church network that helps staff a Christian counseling center, and then I asked who might be available on Thursday at noon. I was fully prepared for not a good fit and having to try again. But as luck—no, as *faith*—would have it, I walked into the room and found the exact person I needed to make sense of my puzzle pieces.

She talked to me about codependency and emotional attachment and other psychological terms you can read whole books about. But for me it boiled down to these two ideas: the mirror and permission. She explained to me that I'd spent a large portion of my life mirroring the emotions of others. It's like empathy, but not really. Empathy is good. Empathy is one of my superpowers. Empathy is being able to feel what other people feel so that you can move toward understanding them. But mirroring—that's when the feelings of other people become the boss of you. When you reflect all their emotions because you've swallowed them whole and let them become your own emotions, too. That is not good.

The people around us are entitled to their feelings. They're entitled to feel tired or frustrated (sometimes with us) or angry or thrilled. And when we empathize, we walk alongside their emotions and we appreciate them. But what don't we do? *We don't own those emotions as our own.*

For a long time, I have owned everyone else's emotions like a boss. Take it from me—it's exhausting and disorienting. It makes you lose your sense of identity and feel lost and unable to decide when you're allowed to feel happy or allowed to feel sad or allowed to disagree, because you've gotten your own feelings so confused with someone else's. You forget that you're allowed to feel entirely differently.

That brings me to permission—the kicker for me. The people pleaser in me keeps waiting for someone to give me permission to take a break, to be off duty. But kids don't know how to do that. They're not wired that way. Kids are consumers. They consume our time and energy, and it's up to the grown-ups to set boundaries and time-outs so we can refuel. Some friendships are like that too. And sometimes, unintentionally, so is marriage.

I didn't know that's what I was doing—running on the feelings and pleasing of others. No one taught me how to stop, because no one taught me how I'd started. And no one taught Peter how to share his inside story with his wife.

For some of us it comes naturally; others are not sure how to translate what's going on inside their heads to those of us on the outside. Maybe they don't even realize they need to. Peter's rich inner life was completely foreign to me. I'm a verbal processor, so whatever he didn't say, I assumed wasn't happening.

If he wasn't saying it, then I didn't know that he was wrestling with the stress of grading deadlines or planning entire new designs for his courses or resenting all the time, energy, and money the three koi ponds in our garden were eating up. So on a Sunday afternoon as I was puttering around the kitchen, making cookies with the kids and folding laundry, I asked for his help to go pick up a kid from a friend's house and found myself stunned to be met with a wall of solid resistance and his own anger at being stretched past his max. What I thought was just a chatty conversation and a casual afternoon errand turned into a growling indictment of how little I appreciated the kind of pressure he was under.

The only time his inside thoughts used to come out into the light of day was either when he was so frustrated that I had requested what he couldn't give, or anytime we were on vacation with his family. When his parents would ask him how work or life or the koi were, I would get to hear him lay out months of what had been going on inside his head. And what I overheard often surprised me.

I started to tease that the best way for me to know what was up with him at work or in his faith or his dreams was to wait for family vacations when he was forced to share updates. I joked about it, but I never realized there might be something we could do about it. Together. It was just who he was. And who I was—the partner who kept the house running and the calendar chugging along. Even the kids knew that Mom was the one who always knew the plan and that Dad was the fun one.

So I started screaming at Peter before that Facebook Live because I was so exhausted from being the plan maker and plan carry-out-er and wait-er on permission to just get a break from it all. But no one ever gave me a break, and I was tired of being the grown-up by myself. I wanted my best friend and partner to come pick up the part of the plan I was tired of hauling around. I wanted him to tuck our daughter into bed beside him that night, smile, and send me back out into the living room to do my job, knowing that he was picking up all the slack on the other side of the screen.

And when he didn't—when he didn't give me permission to focus on my work, when he didn't give me permission to finally call it quits after a long day of managing the house and all the people in it, when he didn't let me into his head so I could understand how our lives looked from his two-hours-each-way daily commute and stressful spreadsheets—all my unexpressed and unexplained panic came charging out my mouth until my throat burned. It was like bile, and I vomited it all up until the last words slammed out and into him: "And now you've made me totally freak out and lose it before I'm supposed to go host this conversation like a good Christian author and you don't even care how you've made me feel!"

And there it was: neither of us had the keys to understanding each other. Sure, for whole seasons we'd diligently remember to pass them back and forth and willingly unlock who we were, but years roll by and locks change and it takes intentionality in a marriage to keep making copies of the keys to all your secret places and handing them over to someone else. It starts to feel like work. Because it is work.

My counselor let me in on a secret: *Peter* didn't make me feel anything; *I* did.

I just have to sit with that for a while.

Peter is not the boss of my feelings in this marriage. He's certainly a steward of them. He's a caretaker of my feelings and a trusted and kind counselor of them. He's a rock when it comes to them, and he's a safe place to share them, but he's not the boss of them.

I have become convinced that even *I* am not supposed to be the boss of my own feelings. Instead, I'm supposed to entrust them entirely to God's Holy Spirit and invite that ultimate counselor in to shape and transform my feelings into something that can be trusted and safe. Because He promises to remake me into the most beautiful version of who He sees me as.

So after a counseling appointment one day, after surviving that Facebook Live, after seeing myself with new eyes, I turned up our gravel lane and sat in the minivan in the late-afternoon sunshine with the engine running and Kesha on the radio singing "Praying." Then I turned off the car and went into the house to find Peter and give him the key to me. To give him the key to understanding why I screamed and why I will likely keep screaming if I don't let him into the secret rooms in my head, where I am finally starting to unlock who I am.

Here at the middle place of my life, I am finally able to look back and make sense of most of the beginning. The confusing, weird beginning where you go from being a daughter to a new wife to a new mom and you make mistakes and get shaped by other people's mistakes and start to feel lost or like you've hit a dead end. But maybe finally one day when you've spent time studying the map some more, when you've got your bearings, you creak a door open and take a long look around and realize that your mind's secret nooks and crannies aren't as dark or scary as you once thought.

Instead, you throw open the windows and wipe dust off the window seats and lean out to catch a great gulp of fresh air, and then you invite your husband in to sit down beside you. And when he actually does, it's such a tender gift that you want to cry. When he sits down long enough to hear you explain about mirrors and permission and how you plan to set yourself free, you can actually feel the release.

So Peter and I sat and talked, and I asked for his own keys. I asked to be invited into his head instead of being a stunned bystander anytime information trickled out. Because how can I comfort or connect or cheer when I don't know? And how can he support and listen and give me space for rest when I don't ask for it?

So I started to ask, and he started to share, and slowly we made ourselves at home in each other's rooms where we hadn't spent time before. The new rooms that are constantly, unknowingly, added on to the spaces of our lives. Those ever-always fixer-uppers. Now when I feel the tension building in him, I know to ask, "What's actually going on inside your head right now?" rather than internalizing the tension and resenting him for it without saying a word.

I also know to tell myself, "You're allowed," when I'm steaming over the hot sink and it's late and all I want to do is catch a show before I'm too exhausted. I sometimes say it out loud. I give myself permission to exhale. To move to the sofa before all the dishes are cleared, better yet to assign that chore to the kids. I tell my children, "Okay, pals, you're up. Mama's on a break now." And then I mean it.

And I have a husband who backs me up. I hear him through the hall door, his voice drifting to where I'm napping on a Sunday afternoon: "No, Zoe, Mommy's napping. What do you need? I can help you." And I know he means it. And I snuggle deeper into the covers because I'm off duty and I don't feel guilty about it. He has the key.

Last week as he walked into the house, I told him I needed to go drop something off at the post office. We passed each other and handed off the parenting baton, and after the post office, I texted and said I was going to swing by the grocery store and then the bookstore real quick too. And my heart chugged a little faster and I reminded myself that I'm a grown-up and it's okay to be out a little longer than planned. The dad's in charge and I don't need to baby him or humor him, but I can make this decision to take an hour extra without the world imploding.

And then my phone pinged as a message came in. I looked down at his words, and a grin split my face open and the sun streamed into the car even though it was overcast and snowing outside: "Hey, hon, kids are all doing great here. Take your time. No need to rush back. You have permission to take as long as you want."

I laughed out loud as I buckled my seat belt and warmth flooded through me because he knows I don't need his permission. He knows that what I need is to be understood. He gave me the words that make me feel the most understood—because I gave him the key. So I started the car, put on the turn indicator, and swung out into traffic with the heater blasting and my heart warming up the whole space between us.

Ordinary Is Sexy

I'm so done letting the movies define what romance looks like! I'm tired of love having to be spelled out in spectacular YouTube-worthy proposals or promposals or whatever the kids are doing these days. Here in my comfy forties, I'm 100 percent sold out on the idea that ordinary is 100 percent where sexy lives.

Pete and I will celebrate twenty years married this year, but good gracious, I'm so glad it's not beautifully posed, cropped, and filtered engagement photos that define love stories. It's all the decades that come next that are the glue of commitment.

I mean it.

Give me an ordinary love.

Give me morning hair and comfy old pajama pants.

Give me dirty socks next to the bed we're together in every night. Even if the bed is on different continents at different times and seasons of life. Even if the bed sags in the middle. Even if the bed is full of long, growing limbs and tiny, precious bad dreams that need to be comforted with blind kisses.

Give me an ordinary love.

Even on its most boring days.

Give me an ordinary love.

Give me a dishwasher unloaded without fail every morning, noon, and night.

Give me basketball practices he never misses and boys he always listens to.

Give me Lego patience and Polly Pocket fascination.

Give me an ordinary love.

Give me sticky kisses over South African pancakes and dreams we worry over side by side. Give me spreadsheets that project our future, and tiny humans who clamber up and into our laps and laugh us away from our columns and into their bright-blue skies of tomorrow.

Give me an ordinary love.

Give me tiny feet on top of big black dress shoes.

Give me pizza on Friday nights and hamburgers the way he makes them.

Keep your magazines and movie endings and mad dashes through airports. Just give me an ordinary love.

Give me a love that I can touch and hold and snort out loud with, that I can fight and fume and cry with, that I can trust and hope and dream with, that I can warm my feet up against under the covers at midnight.

Give me an ordinary love.

Even on its most boring days.

Give me an ordinary love.

Keep your perfect endings and Pinterest pretty and give me un shaved on Saturday mornings, surrounded by the clutter of the week before and a good sense of humor as that same Disney princess movie sings over and over again in the background.

Keep your rom-com expectations and give me the man who wipes snow off my windshield with a dish towel because I can't find the scraper.

Keep your chocolates, flowers, and one-day-a-year calendar countdowns and give me someone who folds the laundry and sleeps in the bottom bunk on stormy nights of bad dreams because his sons believe that dads can punch bears.

(I'll take your tulips, though.)

Give me an ordinary love.

One I can kiss and hold and grow old with. Unselfconsciously.

Give me an ordinary love that believes in commitment.

Give me an ordinary love that isn't afraid of change. Of wrinkles. Of this shaped-by-children waist.

Give me an ordinary love that sees my reflection in the eyes of my children and loves me just the way I am.

Give me an ordinary love.

Give me an ordinary love that changes batteries and light bulbs, that drives the old car and mixes up the basketball times, that believes in the God of his father and mother and passes down the old stories to his sons and his daughter.

Give me an ordinary love.

Give me an ordinary love.

Give me an ordinary love.

Because with him, I'm who I want to be.

To the Father of My Children

*I*didn't know to expect this. I didn't know to expect how much our kids would love you and what that would do to the lenses I watch you through. We were kids ourselves for so long. Kids who got it wrong and hurt each other and disagreed and then stumbled our way into parenthood while we were stumbling our way back to life overseas. What a crazy combination of time zones that brought our children into the world.

But look now. Look how they love you!

Did you know? Did you always know how Zoe would stroke your beard and lean into the curve of your belly and make herself at home in that spot between your shoulder and your hip on the sofa while you watch some new dance show with her? Did you know that you would be her first love story, the one she'd measure all other boys against? I didn't.

I didn't know that at 2 a.m. when Jackson came into our room trying to shake free of his bad dreams in the comfort of our bed on a night when Zoe was already there buried deep into my side, you would simply relocate with him to his bed. You would pick up your pillow and your warmth and would walk down the dark hallway to crawl into a twin bed so that your son could feel his dad's presence pushing back the shadows with each breath and each snore and each arm wrapped around him.

I didn't know that you would study our kids the way you researched your PhD. That you'd learn their unique love languages and sink time and energy you didn't always have into reaching each of them in wildly different ways. I have watched you wade into our freezing-cold koi ponds on early spring mornings because Micah had been counting down the weeks till he'd be working with you in the yard again. You've clocked hours, scooping and power washing and teaching him how to check the air pumps and balance how much food is given and clean the filters. You've pushed back against your natural inclination, which is the same as mine: to spend most weekends on the sofa with a book or a good movie or a sports game. Instead, you've invested in our son. You've bet all your time on him and I've watched the payoff multiply weekend after weekend.

I've heard the awe in his voice every time you let him take one more step toward his great ambition of learning how to drive the riding mower. I've overheard snatches of instruction as it's blown across the yard on the breeze of exhaust fumes and fresh-cut grass and in through the front door as I'm washing dishes or napping in the bedroom. You keep teaching and teaching, patiently pouring words and attention into this son of ours who loves by doing. You have become a doer, against your own nature and inclination. You have spent hours doing together. Did you know that you'd teach a ten-year-old how to drive the mower he lovingly calls "John D"? Or that even on the Sunday afternoons when you didn't feel like it, you'd be out in the yard with him raking up grass clippings and leaves while the middle child who shares your name in the middle of his shared a conversation made up of a thousand questions a minute?

Did you know you'd learn all the latest minutiae about the lives of soccer players you grew up never caring about? Did you know you'd research indoor and outdoor soccer cleats or that you'd dream up a trip for a thirteenth birthday to the soccer stadiums of Europe because that's where your firstborn's imagination lives? I didn't. I didn't know that the man I married, the man so squeamish about medical procedures that he couldn't handle a conversation about LASIK eye surgery without his face signaling physical pain, would one day be coaxing your hysterical middle schooler to let you swipe your finger across his eye to find the stray contact lens that had gone missing after a long, sweaty afternoon on the pitch. How he was freaking out because he couldn't find the lens despite all he and I had done to try to set it free. So it was you who came into the room to calm him down when I'd backed away from his red, frustrated face. When I couldn't bear his pain and didn't know how to fix it. It was you he would allow to try to extract that rogue lens with your big fingers so tenderly wiping at your son's eye. Did you know you'd be the one to load your weeping boy into the car and race him to the optometrist before closing hour to get the lost lens found and how not once did you ever comment on how shocking it was to you to be exploring the interior of your son's eyelids?

You have famously told me and, when they were old enough, told our children, "There is nothing about my kids that grosses me out." And you've meant it. You can't stand opening the cans of wet cat food, but you have cleaned up kid diarrhea and vomit and blood and urine, and you've always, always honored them by how you've done it.

These are the things you don't know when you say your wedding vows. When you dress up in a tux and layer upon layer of lace and shiny shoes and makeup and smiles, and you can't possibly know that your husband will one day be capable of loving your children in the messiest of ways that make you gag while simultaneously making your heart race. How love keeps saying "I do" at midnight when the washing machine is set on repeat and the stomach bug keeps roaring. And at 7 a.m. on baseball photo days and at 9 p.m. when football practice goes late into the rain and Dad is there in the stands waiting.

Did you know that your daughter would talk you into doing interpretive dance with her? Did you know that a tiny seven-year-old would boldly tell you over and over again when to spin, when to lift her in the air, when to twirl, and when to sweep her off her feet? Did you know she'd make you perform that routine for everyone you're related to and you'd do it without even cracking a smile? You'd do it, matching her serious commitment to her art, and you'd dance with love and abandon and melt her heart and mine.

Did you know you'd watch YouTube tutorials about how to coach Little League baseball, how to measure soil erosion for a science project, and how to train up-and-coming basketball players? Did you know you'd rush home through gridlock traffic to trade your suit for those beat-up old jeans and baseball cap and show up at the sidelines to coach your boys through baseball and basketball and offer advice and encouragement at the side of every soccer pitch? Did you know how much Zoe would love being the coach's daughter, and did you know you'd always make time to steal a hug with her on the side of the baseball field in between innings? Did you know you'd get to know coaches and parents and that season after season you'd take your boys shopping for new shoes, despite your wife's balking at the cost? Did you know how much it would delight you to say all those yeses to all those cleats that brought Jackson to tears of joy?

I didn't.

I didn't know there would be this whole other dimension to how I love you.

A love that looks like the grins on our kids' faces when they see you there cheering for them. When they want to know what you thought of how they played and you've always got enthusiasm and thoughtful feedback. How there is no game or loss or disappointment or failure that leaves you without something encouraging to say. How you have become the voice in their heads when they step onto the field or court or dance recital floor. I remember the time I looked over at you as you sat in the dark theater beside me as your tiny daughter came onto the stage in her tutu and headdress. And there you were, like you promised, on time and straight off the sidelines of the playoff baseball game, holding a bouquet of roses in one hand and the protective cup one of your sons had given you to hold in the other.

This is how you father—without embarrassment and with total commitment. Your kids believe in you. They believe that you will always show up when you say you will. They believe you when you tell them you believe in them. And then they set out to prove you right, whether it's on the sports field, a spelling test, or that essay they had to write. They believe they can because their father believed it first.

Did you know how much you'd mean to the children you and I never knew to expect?

Did you know you'd spend hours each and every early morning adding a forty-five-minute detour to your work commute in order to drive your oldest son to middle school? And that when I ached for you having to spend all those extra hours in the car, you'd simply tell me, "When else would I have an hour alone every day with my teen son to simply be together and talk about whatever he wants to?" And I smile every time I think about the two of you setting off before the sun is even up and I pack his lunch and make him hot tea as he gets ready to step into the day with his father by his side.

And did you know at the end of long days that your hands, your baseball mitt–sized hands, would be the safest place for our kids to end up? The place where they'd take their report cards and cuts and scrapes, their fears, their bad dreams and their secrets and failures too. That your hands would hold them and soothe them and pat backs and slap high fives and tuck them under covers.

I didn't know what I didn't know. I don't think you did either. But I sure like unwrapping this gift that neither of us knew to expect, together.

Part 3

Why the Middle of Your Parenting Matters

Parenting Is Do-Overs Times Infinity

I can't find my firstborn anywhere and I'm equal parts terrified and furious. I just got done yelling at him and shaming him and then slammed myself into my bedroom to calm down. When I come back into the living room, he's gone. He's not in his bedroom or bathroom. He's not hiding in a closet or behind a door anywhere. I walk into the yard and scream his name. It echoes back to me like a slap in the face, and I can feel my heart pick up the pace.

I stomp back inside in my brown boots and self-righteousness, and my head is throbbing because I'm so mad at him. And so desperate to find him. I don't want to call his dad and share my worry because then I'd also have to share what I don't want to admit I said. So I keep pacing back and forth between rooms and yelling, and it's making me angrier and angrier, and I now also feel like I want to throw up.

He wouldn't have run away, would he? There's nowhere really to go. We're at the end of an old gravel lane, and everyone in this small community is pretty much related. He wouldn't be stupid enough to risk walking out of here onto the fast-paced, no-sidewalk main road. Would he?

I'm slamming his bathroom door and demanding his name, when

I hear the front door clack closed. I can feel my pulse spike and then start to slow down. I don't recognize how hard the fear was pounding until it withdraws. He walks in but won't look at me. I don't know where to start. *I am right and he is wrong. He is an almost-teenager and I am the grown-up.* This is what I know. *He is disobedient and I am determined to be respected.* This I know.

But he doesn't look like someone who has learned something worth respecting; he looks like someone who has just learned his mother can't be trusted. I'm clenching my fists. *He's the one who can't be trusted,* a whiny voice in my head insists. I'm trying really hard to remember that I'm the grown-up, and I'm trying to figure out how a grown-up would act in this situation.

The world of YouTube and Snapchat and really all the online things are like walking through the African bush, never knowing what is waiting out there for you. But the one thing we drill into our kids' heads is, "You do not go into the bush alone; you always take a parent."

Today he didn't. He went walking through big-game country online without me. He hopped the virtual security fences we have and then tried to hide it from me. And I'm not even talking porn here. Thank God he didn't go stumbling into that minefield. But he went down a few rabbit trails—harmless on the surface, sure, but always leading nowhere good. I'm so furious at his recklessness that I can hardly see straight. I am so furious that I forget to listen. I forget that he doesn't know all the things I know.

So I vented like a fool. The more venom that poured out of me, the more I watched my son shrink right there in front of me. He wanted to become invisible and so he did. It's when I walked away to cool off that he disappeared.

Parenting is always like finding yourself back at the beginning. Just when you think you've earned your PhD in newborns, your baby is a toddler and you're back to the basics of what that means. Then you graduate out of that stage, finally feeling you've got things figured out, just in time to hit the elementary-school years, where you're back to the drawing board. And here we are again, taking baby steps into the tween and teen years, and I keep falling down.

When he's finally back in the house and I can't figure out anything helpful to say, I give us both a time-out. I'm panicked at how little I know about this stage, so I finally call Peter. I call and confess how mad I am and how justified I am at feeling mad, and Peter listens to all of it. He listens and then asks me, "Do you know how much Jackson loves you?"

I'm not sure how to reply.

Pete keeps talking.

"When we drive home from school, he talks about you a lot. These days he talks about how he can't seem to make you happy."

My gut tightens.

"He wants to make you proud, but you're so quick to pick him apart."

I know this is true. I don't want to know it, but I know it. I hate that I know it.

"He is trying to figure out how to talk to you these days without you jumping straight to the part where you point out what he did wrong or should have done differently. Did you listen to him today? Did you try to understand how he got to the decision you disapproved of instead of just jumping up and down on the decision itself?"

I know I didn't.

"He's still only twelve, hon," my husband gently reminds me. "He needs you. And he needs you to give him the benefit of the doubt."

When did I become this perfectionist taskmaster? I try to trace the path in my mind; I try to map out when I went from being his champion to being his judge. I think it was when he changed schools this year, when he started middle school. I went from being an easy-breezy parent to being a crazed helicopter maniac the moment I got my login ID to be able to access his grades and homework assignments in real time. I started to obsess. I started to stalk his due dates and constantly nag when he missed points or deadlines.

I wasn't his mom; I was the new girl who needed her kid to fit in so *she* could fit in. Somehow his grades had become my grades, and his decisions my decisions. He was my reflection, and I hated when the reflection didn't look the way I wanted.

So I crunched down on him. I crunched and pressured and threatened and cajoled, and then when he still made decisions that were inexplicable to me, I unleashed the shame hydrant.

Peter gently points this out, gently but firmly.

I shrink from hearing it, but I know it's true. I also know where I inherited it. In the time between my mom's death and my father's remarriage to the woman who healed us all, there were years of shame. Years of his words that cracked like a whip.

And now here I am sitting at the foot of my bed with my legs crossed under me, ear pressed up to the phone, listening to my husband paint the picture of the parent I never wanted to grow up to be. I breathe in and out through my mouth. I trace the pattern of the carpet with one finger. I know it's not a life sentence. I know it's just a choice. I can choose to be a different parenting story for my son. I know this because it's what my father did.

My father gradually, deliberately, by the desperate grace of a God who doesn't quit us even when we quit Him, started to change. That mighty, never-giving-up God started to change my father from the inside out. Slowly. But radically. Until just two years ago when we were home visiting and I was nervous to leave my dad in charge of my kids while Peter and I were away for a night. Because my middle child, my Micah, is the reflection of my father's own passion and stubbornness and temper. I worried about the combination of the two of them— what the combustion would look like if I weren't there to mediate. But Dad and Wanda, his remarkable wife, sent us packing, and off we went.

Days later I heard the story of what didn't surprise me: Micah's behavior had run amok, and warning after warning had no effect until, my dad later told me, they had to put him in time-out. At this point in my dad's retelling of the story, my tummy bunches up and I regret having left and kinda want to cut the story short so I can go check on my kid. But then I hear what my dad is saying, and my mouth slowly falls open.

"But being in a time-out is a hard thing for a little guy," my dad is saying. "I thought it must be lonely to be left out of all the fun, so I went to find him in the bedroom."

My dad is standing in the hallway between the kitchen and the wide expanse of the dining room table as he tells me the story. Peter and I are standing, fascinated, listening to him. This man whose temper defined my entire childhood. I can't believe the words that are coming out of his mouth.

"I went in, and he was just sitting on the bed looking at the floor. I sat down next to him and said, 'It must be hard being in here alone. I miss you, my big boy, and I don't want you to be alone. But you can't be with everyone else right now until you can treat them politely again.

So I tell you what, I'm going to be in time-out with you. Okay? I'll just sit right here next to you and we'll be in time-out together.' "

Peter and I are staring at my dad as if he's some alien life-form we've never seen before. I remember that day as if it were yesterday. I remember it as I hear my husband's words in my ears. As I see my other son's face in my mind.

My dad learned to parent with compassion and without shame. He made Micah's consequences his own consequences. They walked through it together. And now Micah has come by his hero worship for my dad honestly. He believes that his oupa knows the answer to any question he can dream up—about the weather, farming, medicine, raising bees. This is what shame-free parenting looks like.

I go find my elder son. He still won't make eye contact with me. I sit down next to him and ask him if he knows what it means to play the shame game. He shakes his head. So I tell him that it's one thing for parents to help their kids make smart choices—that it's good for parents to set limits and consequences for their kids. It's a completely different thing for parents to make their kids feel bad about themselves instead of just about what they've done.

"There's a difference between doing a bad thing and being a bad kid, Jackson," I tell him. "And I'm sorry. I'm so sorry I made you feel like a bad kid. That's not okay. That's never okay."

Slowly, he looks up from the floor and into my eyes. His are red and swimming.

"You have my permission to call me on it," I tell him. "Just like I'm allowed to call you on bad behavior, you're allowed to call me on it when I'm shaming you instead of teaching you."

He nods slowly.

"My job is to be your teacher, Jackson. My job is to help you make good choices by teaching you what those look like. My job is to teach and to figure out how to keep teaching you better when you mess up. To keep giving you more and more tools for all the decisions you will have to make for yourself as you grow up. But if I ever slip into shaming and not teaching, then you better call me on it. You have permission to straight-up say, 'Mom, you're playing the shame game,' and I promise to listen and I promise to learn and I promise to stop and take a breath and try again. Deal?"

He leans his head against me and I hold his body and slowly we both exhale and just sit there on his bed with the comforter that has the galaxy painted on it in vivid blues, and we hold each other. This is what do-overs look like; they hold the whole world in their hands.

Compassion leans in and listens. Fear screams and chases us away. Fear is a terrible teacher and an even worse parent. We sit on the bed together and we do it all over again—the conversation, the questions, and the decisions—and I lean in to try to understand the choices he made online that day. I hold it like so much treasure when he shares with me the parts of what makes a twelve-year old boy tick. I look down at my arms and I'm amazed that he still fits there just as he did when he was born. So much delicate hope packaged in all this beautiful skin.

When our kids are brand new and trusted to our shaky hands, we know with certainty that we would die for them without even pausing for thought. We would walk into dark alleys and offer ourselves as ransom for them without consulting anyone; our instincts would make the decision easy. Yet here we sit, and I'm the one who has hurt him deeper than anyone else. And I'm still the one who can make it better. How is it possible to be trusted with such terrifying power?

Some nights I lie in bed and it's hard to breathe. I used to think newborn sleeplessness was the worst. But I've graduated into elementary and middle school panic, and that age has awoken a whole host of new worries.

Because now they can remember how badly I mess up.

This thought terrifies me. Maybe you are living in that reality right now. The one where your kid is in his room or has stormed out with her friends and you're at the computer wishing you could get a take-back.

Lunchables and do-overs seem to be the bread and butter of parenting. But last year I heard a story that's crawled under my rib cage and offered some hope. I heard my favorite author of books about boys tell the story of a father who'd messed up. Messed up good and proper for years. Messed up more than playing the shame game. Messed up more than just missing a few soccer games and homework assignments. He missed life. For years. Until his three girls were grown and were growing families of their own, reinventing the word without him.

They took for granted the fact that he had checked out of their lives.

That's when he decided to check back in.

When bridges, doors, and expectations all had been burned, that dad whose kids had outgrown him came back for another try.

Trying again is always awkward. It's so uncomfortable to keep trying to find new ways to say, "I love you." And "I'm sorry."

He called all three of his daughters and asked if he could visit them. They were surprised. A lot surprised. They wanted to know what kind of agenda he had. And he said he just wanted to be part of their routine. To fit into the nooks and crannies of their lives so he could understand how they looked from the inside.

The women were skeptical, but they opened their doors anyway.

And their dad? He showed up throughout the year, paying them each a visit. True to his word, he tagged along for everything. He was there for breakfast and car pool and pickup. He watched homework get done and games get squabbled over. He came to sports matches and helped make the macaroni.

He quieted himself so he could hear what was going on in the big wide world of his daughters' lives.

He was present.

He was interested.

And a parent like that is hard to resist, hard to write off.

This dad gives me hope, because he should have been too late. Instead, his girls were fascinated by how fascinating he found them.

On the last night of their do-over weeks together, he would take each daughter out to dinner. Over dessert he asked a question. He asked his grown-up, no-longer-wearing-pigtails, raising-kids-themselves daughters, "What do you dream?"

I was standing in the very back row of the overcrowded hotel conference room and you could have heard a pin drop as two hundred moms let that question run around their heads. In the midst of all our everyday to-dos, it's rare to have someone ask about dreams that may have been lost in a thousand miles of car pool.

He wasn't too late. It turns out that this dad arrived in time to remind his daughters of when they dreamed, wild and free, as only children can. And to show up to champion those long-forgotten dreams.*

You're not too late either.

---

* This was a story told in a workshop by David Thomas at LifeWay's dotMOM event several years ago. He is a coauthor of *Wild Things: The Art of Nurturing Boys* (Carol Stream, IL: Tyndale, 2009).

No matter how hard you fought or slammed that door or disagreed or stormed out or said things you wish you could take back. No matter if you threw his math book across the room or if she declared you the worst mom, like, ever.

You're too late only once you give up going back for another do-over.

You're too late only if you stop trying again.

Too late isn't too late until you walk out and don't walk back in again.

You're too late only if you've run out of tomorrows.

So tonight I will set my alarm and get up ready for fresh do-overs. And maybe doughnuts. It's hard to tell which tastes better.

Sobbing in My Minivan
over Honor Roll

*O*ur middle kid has sat through five years of "success assemblies," where kids are recognized for making honor roll or for leadership or for perfect attendance. And not once, *not once,* in those five years from kindergarten through fourth grade has his name ever been called. Year after year, success assembly after success assembly, he has sat on the floor while all his friends have had their turns to get up and get their certificates.

This is an excruciating kind of torture. To have to sit and watch while the kids around you all stand to the applause of their parents and go forward to be recognized. I know that side, too, because both of my other kiddos have had their fair share of certificates and accolades. But neither of them ever worked as hard as our kiddo in the middle. If you're a mom of a kid with any kind of learning disability or speech disability or any other challenge they've had to overcome in the classroom, you probably know what I mean.

Because you, too, know what it's like for ten minutes of spelling homework to bleed into two hours of tears and gnashing of teeth. You know the profound self-doubt that can swamp a kid. You know the struggle that comes from not being able to make the words that come out of your mouth sound like the words on the page. Of always feeling different or behind or just not smart enough. We've lived it too. We've lived individual education plans and speech therapists and long stretches of struggling to understand the words that came out of our son's mouth.

So many nights of frustration. So many afternoons trying to turn back the tide of our kid's belief that he was stupid. He would sit at the long stretch of the kitchen table with his face screwed up in a fury of self-loathing, tears streaming hot down his cheeks, and the pencil nearly snapping in half as he tried to sound out the words he was supposed to spell but that he could barely pronounce.

My head would throb, my heart would break, and every afternoon as the arrival of the school bus grew closer and closer, I'd feel the slow build of deep anxiety. *Here we go again,* I'd think, and an afternoon of fun and digging in the yard would morph into an evening of torture as we all took turns trying to help Micah through the horror that was his world of spelling and reading.

It started to eat away at my soul. Not that he couldn't spell but that he believed he would never be able to spell. We spent night after night, year after year, with spelling list after spelling list, and by the time Micah reached fourth grade, we finally entered the world of a teacher who believed in him with a conviction that carried weight, and we all caught a fresh breeze of hope. I sat down with her during the very first week of school and gave Ms. Noord the scoop on this kid we love so much. I laid out his phobia about spelling and the posttraumatic stress he experienced anytime he got a new set of words he was sure he was going to flunk . . . again. She listened and she heard, and then she advised and laid out the plan to set him up for success.

What she taught in the classroom, we underlined at home. And what we poured into him at home, she echoed in the classroom. We were a team. And very slowly, Micah started to believe that it might be true. That maybe he wasn't destined for perpetual failure. That maybe he could get that elusive B in spelling.

I was too afraid to hope with him. I admit it. I was so tenderly guarding his newfound faith in his own abilities that I didn't want to weigh them down with any kind of expectations. I just wanted him to keep taking one new step each day. Gradually we were working our way out of the black hole and into a place where his brain had stopped telling him lies about how useless he was and had started storing away new sounds and spelling combinations until he could understand them.

Every night his dad read with him. It was very slow going. Often there were still tears as he would lash out at the book or, on the worst nights, at himself. But we persisted. We signed up for online spelling games. I scoured libraries for books that would pique his interest and then we invested in the entire series. He still sounded out every syllable, but we were making progress. Syllables became words, and words became sentences, and sentences became entire paragraphs, until he could slowly and stubbornly read whole pages at a time.

We believed in him, and Ms. Noord believed in him. And finally he started to believe in himself. And he started to say his dream out loud: "I am *going* to make honor roll this year." He'd say it over and over, as if saying it out loud could make it so. I admit that in a quiet corner of my heart, I never really let myself believe it. I didn't think I could handle my own disappointment alongside his if he missed that mark again. So I cheered and I championed and I was terrified when he told me that report cards were coming home the next day.

Sure, there had been an uptick in his spelling-test scores and he was reading with confidence, even if not always with accuracy. But would this equal a grade higher than the Cs and Ds we were used to? I had no idea. I just know I showed up at the bus stop early. I sat in the minivan with the engine running and the windows cracked open and I waited. So much of parenting is waiting, isn't it? Waiting on first words and first steps and the first time they figure something out for themselves. And then you're off to the races because now they're speeding through so many new things and you're left behind, waiting for them to share, to loop you into the world they're learning to inhabit without you.

So I waited and the sun bled through the watery clouds and the big yellow school bus rolled to a stop at the corner of Forest Avenue. I squinted through the window at the door that had folded open, and my brain tried to catch up with what my eyes were seeing: kids hopping off the bus one by one, blocking my view, and then the biggest boy in the neighborhood standing on the bottom step with his hands held high above his head, clutching a sheet of paper like it was a golden ticket and yelling, whooping really, as loud as he could, "I made honor rollllllll! I did it! I did it!"

Then he was in the car and shoving the paper into my stunned hands as I scanned the grades and then the words in that final paragraph: "Congratulations on making honor roll!"

He really did it! All As and the long-dreamed of Bs, in reading and spelling and comprehension. I almost scared him with my excitement for him. My chest heaved and my eyes filled as I wrapped my arms around him. Because there's no brave like watching our kids be brave. There's no joy like watching them overcome their deepest fears. I hugged Micah tight to my heart in the car, the gearshift poking us weirdly in the ribs, my mascara streaming down my cheeks, tears and laughter mingling, and his eyes were a mirror of my own: disbelief and wonder at the same time.

We drove down the gravel lane to our house, and when he saw that his dad's car was already parked there, already home, he flew out of the car and straight for his father. I caught up to them in the kitchen as Micah waved his report card in the air, and his dad's face caught fire with pride and he braced himself as Micah, our giant boy, launched into his arms. I have a photo of that moment. Of the ecstasy of a nine-year-old boy who knew that his father believed in him and of the joy of a father watching his son grow into his potential.

Their crazy laughter was like a magnet for the rest of the family, and everyone piled on and we were a scrum of celebration. This is why we do the 364 nights of tears and frustration—because we know there is that one day waiting out there to recognize all we have sown. That one day when we get to reap so much delight that we can barely hold it all in our hands.

On success-assembly day, I arrived nearly a full hour early because I was determined to have a front-row seat. And I was a goner from the moment the classes marched in. Micah has zero poker face and kept turning around to wave and grin at me. I tried to remind myself not to spend all my time behind the lens snapping photos but to instead absorb the moment as it happened live. To see it with my own two eyes and let that be the best photo of the day.

Because our last name is Baker, I knew that it would be a short countdown before Micah was called. Finally, finally called to walk up to the podium and receive his award. I sat awkwardly between two parents I didn't know as I clapped so hard that my palms felt raw. "Micah Baker, honor roll," and there he was, standing up. Standing up and walking to the front. And then he was shaking Ms. Noord's hand as she bent down to look him in the eyes, and I watched the grin split across her face and spread onto his.

Then he walked to line up across the front of the hall with his classmates, and he held his certificate above his head and signaled for me to take photo after photo. Some moments can't possibly be recorded enough. So I snapped away at him and cheered and clapped and gave him a thumbs-up, and we had matching grins. But I also had tears and a massive balloon in the place where my heart should have been. It felt as though my chest would burst from the joy of it all.

And when the ceremony was over, I went to find him and wrap him up in my pride, and we both made our way over to the teacher who had been the game changer for all of us that year. I had so many feelings for her that I knew I would have to rein in my crazy and not sob all over her. Because my hands were shaking so much from all my feelings, I could hardly take the photo I so badly wanted of dear, dear Ms. Noord and Micah. If I could put my feelings into words to her, it would sound something like this:

> THANK YOU for always believing in our son. This is the first time in more than FIVE years of school he heard his name called during a success assembly. The first time he didn't have to stay seated through the whole thing. The first time he ever had all As and Bs. Thank you for all you've poured into our kid this year. We know you have a packed classroom and face many challenges, day in and day out. But we know how much you believe in all your kiddos. So thank you. Those seem like really small words. But they come with five years of gratitude. You are our hero.

It's taken us *years* to get here. Years of nightly spelling review. Of frustration and speech therapy and reading tutors and tears. Of giving up and trying again. Of him thinking he'd never master spelling or reading.

But here we are today. I'm trying really hard not to embarrass him with tears. Instead, I'm taking him home early today. For milkshakes. And the reminder that his determination to never, never, never give up got us to this moment today.

So off we went to grab mint-chocolate-chip milkshakes and relive the moment over and over again. I don't know if I will ever take that report card off the fridge. Because no matter what comes next, our boy has this moment. He has the assurance that he is just as capable as anyone else. That he has the hard work, the determination, and the grit not to quit. That not quitting is what success looks like.

To all my fellow moms walking the long road of helping kids overcome learning challenges, please know I think you are the biggest kind of brave. May your faithfulness be celebrated and your kids know that they are phenomenal! Because theirs is the bravest kind of brave: the brave of the long road of perseverance.

What You Don't Know About Parenting

*Y*ou don't know what you don't know about parenting until the moment you're faced with your total ignorance. You feel paralyzed by the weight of what is happening and your complete loss at how to respond. You can't prepare for it. You can just hope to survive it and learn from it. I had zero clue that was how the Christmas program was going to go down last year.

"Dancing is my passion!" our girl declared to the row of friends seated with her on the bus. They were coming back from a school field trip, and her chaperone filled me in later on the no-holds-barred exuberance of our spotlight-loving girl. I laughed and nodded, because I've heard it many times before.

It was our church's Christmas program, and when requests first went out for kids who wanted to participate, Zoe had a full-on squealing freak-out of excitement. This was going to be her first real chance to step onto a stage. She would get to dance! There would be costumes! And ribbons! And makeup! It was months of gleeful rehearsals and afternoons spent practicing her routine, thanks to YouTube videos made by her dance teacher, Ms. Michelle.

All her besties were also part of the dance crew. For weeks they all showed up after church with their packed lunches and enthusiasm to practice and twirl and try not to fray their teacher's nerves, until their parents came to collect them after sometimes sneaking in a few errands or an afternoon nap. Over and over again we were treated to her demonstration of the routine, and over and over again we all dutifully cheered while trying to still watch the TV she was blocking with her waving arms.

She was ready. She was more than ready. There would be a dress rehearsal and two full performances and she talked me into learning how to do a real ballet bun for the big debut. We went to CVS together and scanned all the shelves until we found the Bun Maker, which looked like a mini doughnut designed to hold soft wispy hair into the shape of a solid ballet bun. We snagged the last one with delight and bought packs and packs of bobby pins and then came home to transform her. She was wrapped in her pink robe and standing on her pink bathroom stool as I prayed for God to have mercy on me and help turn it all into a halfway decent bun.

As I ran my hands through my daughter's soft curls, I had tender flashbacks of my own mom trying to sculpt my hair into a 1920s flapper look for my high school musical. My prayers were mercifully answered and the doughnut held and the hair wrapped around it. And miracle of miracles, it looked like a gorgeous, real-life, prima-ballerina-worthy bun! We added two tiny barrettes glittering with fake diamonds and a swipe of lipstick. And then because she pleaded with huge eyes for more makeup on this special occasion, I gave in and added a small swipe of mascara to her already long lashes, with the wand that made her face light up with the magic of all little girls discovering the fun of dress-up.

Her father and brothers dutifully oohed and aahed in admiration at every part of her costume, from her bun to her tiny toes in their stockinged feet. Then she and I were off to church early for the dress rehearsal. On the way, she told me that her stomach felt funny and she wanted to know how many people would be watching her. I made light of the question, as moms do, and focused her attention back on the picture-perfect bun that was poised on top of her head and the fun of being with friends. Then I turned up the tunes and kept up a jolly attitude as she continued to describe the symptoms of what I thought were just a gut full of first-time butterflies.

Arriving helped. Her friends were all at about the same full-throttle-level excitement and there were costumes to be tried on and adjusted and mirrors to admire their reflections in. The decibel level in the tiny dressing room was ear splitting, and nothing could tame the wild thrill of eight girls in the throes of being the center of attention. A roomful of baby girl angels all preparing with the wildest of giggles and yelps to dance in the Christmas program.

When they were all wrapped in angel robes with tiny, delicate headdresses of white and silver flowers and with ribbons attached to their tambourines, they swept into the church sanctuary to take their places for the dress rehearsal. The hall was dark and the only faces were the ones of the choir behind them. The seats were an empty smile of anticipation, and our daughters flooded the stage with their delight, their dance, and their thrill at being able to celebrate Christmas in this tangible way.

I have a photo of Zoe from that afternoon. Her face is ablaze with excitement, and her arms are fluttering above her head, the streamers from her tambourine shining, the choir in the background. She's in her element. And my heart was in my throat watching her. I couldn't look away, she was shining so bright.

We'd sprayed hair and pinned tunics and practiced and calmed precious nerves, and watching them, all I could think was, *My word. Our daughters are preparing to dance for the King of kings. My word.* And I was certain that heaven was holding its breath and leaning over to soak in the earth and the chorus of worship rising like stunning incense from a troop of tiny angelic beings.

Our daughters danced with innocent confidence and the music soared behind them and no one forgot their steps and everyone beamed out at the dark auditorium and danced for the joy of the dancing. Not for applause or approval but for the Christ child, who surely must have been dancing with them. It was so impossible not to imagine His angels up there in our daughters' shoes.

That's why I wasn't prepared. That's why I didn't know what to do when none of the rehearsal translated into the actual performance. They'd trooped offstage and snacked for dinner and calmed down and then got wound up all over again at the anticipation of the real thing.

Her dad and brothers had arrived. They'd brought roses. And we'd promised her we'd sit in the very front row so she could see us. I'd saved seats with my purse and a notebook and a program, and I knew it was an act of love for Peter to willingly sit front and center, but sit we all did with months' worth of anticipation.

But as the program began and the clock ticked closer to their dance number, I looked over at where the flock of little angels was sitting in the sanctuary. Waiting their turn. And Zoe's teacher waved me over with a panicked hand and I found my daughter bent over in terror with tears streaming down her face. My heart went cold as I knelt close so I could hear her words whispered over the choir and the storytelling and into my ear.

"I can't breathe," she croaked.

So I loosened her robes and adjusted her buttons and put my lips right up to her ear to whisper encouragement and soft jokes to shake her out of her worry and back into the picture of confidence I'm used to. But it was like sinking sand, and the tighter I tried to hold her hand, the deeper I watched her sink into her panic. I felt frozen, unable to decide what to do. Should I pull her out? Would she be disappointed afterward if she didn't get to realize her dream with her friends on that stage? My mind was flashing hot and cold as I tried to keep my voice light and my assurances confident that once she got up onstage, she would forget all her fears and would love every minute. She believed me. She held my hand in a death grip and she believed me that somehow it would be okay.

But I was wrong. The lights dimmed and the music played and all the angels flew with the pitter-patter of tiny toes up onto the stage, and when they were lit up again by lights and music, I could see how terribly wrong I was.

My daughter stood in her spotlight, front and center of the stage, desperately singing while tears poured down her face. They weren't light tears and they weren't easy to overlook—they were a storm of terror painted down her cheeks in the hard black stripes of mascara I'd let her wear. I felt as if I were watching a nightmare I couldn't wake her up from. Her panic was like a living thing dancing next to her on the stage. And her face was frozen in a terrible attempt at a smile, but the tears, the tears kept pouring out of her.

I didn't know what to do. I didn't know if I should grab her off the stage and rescue her or if she would be upset that I'd caused an even bigger scene. I didn't know if she wanted to hide or if she wanted to try to finish with head held high. I sat paralyzed on the chair in the front row with my nails cutting lines into my palms and watched a piece of my soul crumple on the stage in front of me.

Parents around us were leaning forward in their seats. I could feel them rooting for her. I could sense the waves of empathy rising to meet her, and still she cried and still she danced and still I sat frozen, unsure what to do. A desperate wreck of emotions and choices, unable to process what was short-circuiting through my brain. Peter's big hand wrapped around my own and I knew we were both stuck in indecision as the choir sang, "Glory to God in the highest."

The second the music stopped and the dancers stepped off the stage with their streamers and headbands full of flowers in bloom, I swept our daughter up and into my arms and down the long aisle and out of the room. She was gasping and grabbing at her neck and choking on her words: "I can't breathe. I can't breathe."

In one desperate tug, I wrenched her costume open, pins and buttons scattering, and stripped her down to her tank top so that she could breathe and escape what had been happening inside her. And the sobs came harder and the fear spilled into words that she kept crying into my ear: "There were so many people watching me. All those people were looking at me."

I held her and rocked her and rubbed her back through her tiny black tank top and slowly, slowly reminded her what she knows to be true—that she is loved no matter what. "Zoe, we love you. We love you. We love you." I repeated it like an anthem as she cried and wiped at her eyes and I passed her handfuls of tissues. But the black streaks down her cheeks wouldn't come off, and the panic still had tight hold of her as we sat in the ladies' bathroom on the pink and maroon sofa with the mirror watching in the background.

I doubt all my choices from that night. I wish I had protected her better from that fear. Fear I didn't even know to anticipate. I wish I had wrapped her up and hidden her offstage. I'm riddled with doubt every time I relive that evening because I don't know if we can ever actually protect our kids from their own fears. Maybe all we can do is show them how brave they are to face them.

Her heart slowly found its way back to its everyday rhythm and I changed her into soft, comfortable, familiar clothes. Then I held her face between both my hands and looked into her dark eyes. I needed her to hear me with more than her ears; I needed her soul to absorb my words because I could see the embarrassment creeping into her head. "Zoe, listen to me. There is absolutely nothing to be embarrassed about tonight. All I saw on that stage is the bravest girl I know."

She tucked her head into the crook of my shoulder and shook it fiercely no. She was crying again. "Listen to me," I said. "I am your mother and I know you better than anyone else does. What you did tonight was incredibly hard and terribly scary, and that's what makes you so brave."

I got only those words out before the door opened and all her friends came trooping into the room, all trying to wrap their arms around her at once. It's the most generous gift, this unrestrained friendship determined to soothe and encourage at the same time. Each trying to say in their own precious way what they thought was bravest about her that night. Each leaning in to assure her that all anyone saw was her courage.

I watched as her face tweaked a hesitant smile, her cheeks expanding across the streaks of mascara that I couldn't seem to properly rub away. But her smile erased those stains and we all watched her for signs of fear or panic or the beginnings of beating herself up. And there was a wall of safe words already forming around her to protect her from any of those lies. That's what love does—it builds a safe place for our healing. I watched my daughter, surrounded by the women she and her friends will grow up to be, as they offered her their own courage while she was still looking for hers.

And at the very end when everyone had changed back into regular clothes and started drifting out of the bathroom, Zoe whispered her one remaining fear: that her teacher would be disappointed in her for ruining the show. I knew that wasn't true. But I also knew that it needed to be addressed immediately. So I caught the hand of Ms. Michelle as she was hanging up costumes and straightening up the room. I told her Zoe's fear. And I watched as Ms. Michelle got down on her knees in front of my daughter. As she held my Zoe's face in both palms and looked deep into her eyes, she said, "I am so proud of you, because you just showed a roomful of grown-ups what it looks like to do brave things."

My daughter blinked her eyes. Took a deep breath. Then we gathered our things to go. It wasn't the night either of us had expected. Later, after I'd soothed her cheeks with soft makeup wipes and she was tucked into bed with her flowers in a vase next to her, I needed my own mom, so I called my mom-in-law. I called her so I could cry like the little girl I still feel like on the inside. I cried about how I felt like I'd failed my daughter, how I worried that I'd scarred her. I cried about everything I wish I'd done differently and everything I didn't even understand how to do differently.

And as mothers have always done, she listened and loved me and then encouraged me with the deep understanding born of her own lifetime of learning what you don't know by simply walking through it. This is what we mothers do for each other—we offer our own failures as proof that our sisters and daughters, our nieces and grands, will make it through the perilous journey of mothering too. Because no matter how many books you read or podcasts you listen to, nothing can prepare you for the fall you weren't expecting. And fall we all will, sister. Hope hinges on the hands willing to grab on to us and pull us back out. This is the antidote to the loneliness of motherhood and the lie that we have failed. This willingness to give other mothers our true stories, especially the ones that don't always have happy endings.

So I sat on the old squishy sofa, wrapped in a blanket with the phone pressed to my cheek and finally felt myself let go the breath I'd been holding. There's welcome relief in the words of a mother who's walked her own roads of failure and figured out how to keep walking forward anyway.

We held on to each other across phone lines and miles, and I was comforted by simply being known. In that moment, in that heartache, in that unexpected pothole, I found that I wasn't alone. There was company down there, who'd been there before. Already waiting to show me the way out.

No One Disappoints
Quite Like a Hero

Our kids need heroes. My kids are thirteen, eleven, and eight. They are old enough to long for a hero. They're old enough to have started noticing.

They notice sports stars and singers and tween celebrities.

They see the kids who have their own YouTube channels and videos that get a million hits for putting together a Lego set or unboxing that new toy. Even my eight year-old knows the lingo and lisps in her games of pretend: "Don't forget to click below to subscribe!"

They hunger and thirst for something to believe in that is bigger than their tiny souls.

I believe that's because it's how we're created, how we're designed.

We're created for a God who fills us up with awe and wonder. A God who out of all the infinite galaxies created one small spot; one tiny pocket of perfect oxygen, temperature, and climate where humanity could exist; the pale blue dot that we call home.

I watch my children growing up and looking around them, in awe at the world we've been given, and they hunger and thirst for something that is worth believing in.

I really noticed it for the first time a couple of summers back when my firstborn asked me about his favorite sports star, "Has he done anything bad?"

And at first I didn't get what he meant, because who hasn't done something bad? Who's immune to the crippling brokenness of this world we love, where we all battle our own terrible bad choices every day? But I went back and replayed his brave question over and over, the way parents do. And on a closer listening, I heard what he was really asking: *Can I believe in him? Can I trust him not to let me down?*

Our children long for heroes they can follow. And the internet, the headlines, the YouTube channels with millions of subscribers—they're falling over themselves to give our kids just that.

They want to make Beliebers out of all of us.

And our kids are starting to believe.

In a recent UK study, kids between the ages of five and ten were asked the age-old question "What do you want to be when you grow up?" The study concluded that "the desire for fame and fortune came ahead of professions involving helping the public, including being a fire fighter or a doctor."* Perhaps it's because the terrible lie that lurks beneath fame, beneath this craving to be our own reality show, is that fame and fortune will somehow, some way, make our lives better.

My sons watch the episode of Zac Efron (the kid my eleven-year-old son loves from the *High School Musical* movie series) as he joins Bear Grylls on the survival show *Running Wild*. And Micah is confused. At

---

* Keith Perry, "One in Five Children Just Want to Be Rich When They Grow Up," *Telegraph*, August 5, 2014, www.telegraph.co.uk/news/newstopics/howaboutthat/11014591/One-in-five -children-just-want-to-be-rich-when-they-grow-up.html.

first I'm confused about why he's confused, because I loved watching Bear and Zac. Watching how Bear leans in and listens and encourages a young celebrity in his attempt to carry the terrible weight of fame.

But both my sons are disappointed by the episode. They keep asking me questions I didn't expect. There's one in particular that hurts to try to answer: "But why wasn't Zac happy? He's famous!"

And there it is. The terrible assumption. That fame makes us better than before. Instead of the ugly truth. That fame can cripple us and power break us and money rob us.

We grown-ups can become numb to this reality because we're so used to it. We barely notice the entertainment magazine headlines about the most recent celebrity marriage that's imploded or the teen pop star who went off the rails. Until my son notices it in his *High School Musical* hero and I read the headlines.

News about Subway's most infamous former spokesperson made my hands shake: "Jared Fogle used 'wealth, status, and secrecy' to exploit kids."* So did the predator Larry Nassar. And I'm just one mom trying to make sense of what's been unpacked over never-ending news cycles. We are a nation stunned and sickened, and I am a mom raising kids who are looking for heroes these days, so I have to pay attention. I read and wipe stunned eyes and try to absorb the enormity of the betrayal and the even greater courage of those who stand in the excruciating, unwanted spotlight to tell their stories and expose the truth. I watch and cry, like you did, and I tell my kids in no uncertain terms that fame is not where we go when we're looking for something to believe in.

---

* Crimesider Staff, "U.S. Atty: Jared Fogle Used 'Wealth, Status, and Secrecy' to Exploit Kids," *CBS News,* August 19, 2015, www.cbsnews.com/news/united-states-attorney-jared-fogle-used-wealth-status-and-secrecy-to-exploit-kids.

Neither is the pulpit nor the soccer field, nor the stage nor the movie studios, for that matter. Because if there's one terrible reminder to come out of the Fogle and Nassar cases, the #MeToo and #TimesUp movements, and the fall after fall of faith leaders, it's that power and influence and fame can be a slippery, lying slope. That instead of wielding their influence to protect the vulnerable, our once-upon-a-time heroes have used it to prey on them.

Operating in the shadow of its own spotlight, fame can take advantage. It can defile itself and us. My sons and daughter want heroes, and instead I look around and see sports stars who have long since stopped playing for the love of the game, franchises built on the backs of children, politicians who haven't been the good guys, and the #MeToo movement, which has us shaken down to our very souls. No one is immune, least of all the church.

So often the spotlight distracts us from what was happening when no one was looking. In the ordinary, everyday lives of these people who have made headlines.

Pay attention, my sons. Pay attention, my daughter.

Pay attention to what happens in your ordinary days when the spotlight is turned off. Because we're easily blinded to how people spend their ordinary time, the time that counts and adds up to lifetimes, because we're so distracted by the bright glare of their spotlights.

We can all buy into our own headlines or our own billboards and be easily bedazzled by who others think we are.

But, sons and daughter, it's when the lights click off and you go home, take off your shoes, and start the shower that you will have to look yourself in the mirror and still recognize who you are. The times when no one is watching but you and Jesus are the times that will define you.

Give me your private moments and I'll show you who you are.

And I'll show you whose you are.

Because none of us belong to ourselves.

We are tenants, stewards of every breath we breathe, wholly answerable to the God who breathed life into us.

What I'm trying to say, my kids, is that there is only one famous one. There is a God who made you. And everything else is on loan. None of it is ours. But all of it will have to be answered for. All of how we spent it, sang it, lived it, chose it, spoke it, blamed it, exploited it, fought it, or loved it. We will have to answer for all of it, "for we must all appear before the judgment seat of Christ, so that each of us may receive what is due us for the things done while in the body, whether good or bad" (2 Corinthians 5:10).

It can sound scary. And maybe some days it should. Maybe we forget far too easily the weight of glory that's been entrusted to us. But the good news is that the person we're answering to is the most famous one who deliberately laid down His glory, His power, and His fame for the least of these. That's you, my boys. That's you, my daughter. And me. And Dad. And the neighbor down the road and across the globe. Our God gave up everything His fame entitled Him to so that He could come and know you and love you and free you in person.

So, children of mine, if you truly want to be known, then tuck yourself, your reputation, and your aspirations into the crook of His name. Walk your ordinary weekdays with your extraordinary God and you won't need fame to find meaning or glory to find recognition.

As Oswald Chambers wrote about embracing the everyday versions of ourselves: "It is ingrained in us that we have to do exceptional things for God—but we do not. We have to be exceptional in the ordinary things of life, and holy on the ordinary streets, among ordinary people—and this is not learned in five minutes."[*]

I'm still learning it. I imagine I will be learning it for the rest of my life.

Between my dirty dishes and the mice I can't get out of my kitchen, between my deadlines and late nights reading favorite books, between scraping the mac and cheese out of the pots and starting the dryer again, I am learning that I am known right here and now in this completely ordinary—some might say boring—moment and that is enough.

Come sit by me, kids, on this old saggy sofa at the end of another week and we'll practice looking each other in the eyes. Because all heroes and all hypocrites begin as somebody's son or daughter. Ordinary is our daily bread, necessary for our survival, and all our broken-down disappointments are arrows pointing home.

Because there is only one worth following, and you'll recognize His voice when He calls you by name.

Kids, follow Him.

Especially when it's inconvenient, awkward, or uncool. Keep following Him; always have a mind hungry to learn and a soul open to correction, instruction, and the delight of learning something new. There was a Bible teacher who sat in the front row at a conference one night when I was the keynote speaker. She's written more books and studies than years I've lived, and I watched her take notes. Pen in hand, she put down on paper what she was learning from what I was teaching. It was so shocking that I almost stopped to ask her what on earth I could possibly have said that was worth her recording. It was only later as I kept replaying the absurdity of it that I realized here is a teacher who

---

[*] Oswald Chambers, quoted in Emily P. Freeman, *Simply Tuesday: Small-Moment Living in a Fast-Moving World* (Grand Rapids, MI: Revell, 2015), 39.

has never stopped being a student. She always shows up believing that God has something fresh to teach her, no matter who the messenger is.

Be that kind of student, my sons and daughter. Be that kind of humble, hungry learner. Because you are never going to be able to check off all the knowledge of this world and the next in your own heart and soul and head. So keep remembering to keep learning, even from the most unexpected sources.

Sometimes that person will be your mother. Sometimes that person will be your mother chasing down the school bus to make you apologize to the bus driver. Yes, I remember that day you got off the bus and thought it was funny to tell me how you'd flicked that pencil at the back of the driver's head and then refused to fess up when she asked who'd done it.

I remember how I got you back into the car and down the road, chasing that bus to its next stop so you could awkwardly run behind me as I ran down the side of the bus and rapped my palm on the door to get the driver's attention, her surprised eyes asking me if I was out of my mind. But I was simply ensuring that you would grow up knowing that actions have consequences and that these parents of yours would not be a hiding place for your bad choices. We will always choose light over shadows. We will model the necessary life skill of apologizing, especially when it's awkward, because we are convinced that the very worst thing we could ever do is protect you from the pain of your own consequences.

But we will never let you carry those alone. We will always walk with you as you speak up, admit what you've done, say you're sorry, and pay your debts. We will be with you right there at the very painful center of owning up to who you are and what you've done and then making it right.

These are the days of fallen heroes, because no one is immune from messing up. Kids, pay attention to the ones who aren't afraid of the words "I was wrong." Pay attention to the ones who speak up, who offer generous apologies and then take ownership for their mistakes and figure out deliberate ways to make things right. Being a leader is leading out when it comes to making things right.

So lead, children of mine. Lead out in your sorrys and in your willingness to forgive your siblings, your parents, and sometimes your heroes. Let them climb off their pedestals and into the real world of real loads of laundry and lawns that need to be mowed. Meet them there and you will see them for who they truly are. Step outside the glare of the spotlight so you can see better, and then don't forget to turn around and face yourself in the mirror. Then come meet me again on the sagging sofa and tell me what you saw. I promise to always listen, to bring the hot tea, to tell you all about my own sometimes stupid, sometimes innocent mistakes. And we will tell the truth about ourselves, and this, my children, is how we will be free.

A Promise for My Daughter

I'm tired and she's tired. And she's been weeping with frustration, her face a smudge of red cheeks and snotty trails.

After two sons, I am often surprised by her riot of unpredictable emotions. I go down on my knees beside her and she is glaring hot blue eyes into my face. I reach for her and she swats at me and doesn't accept the comfort I know she wants.

I gently take her hands and pull her up. Her tender self, all frustration and sweat and vulnerability, melts into me. I cup her with my arms and my words and slowly stroke those damp curls back from her cheeks.

I've got deadlines and to-do lists and no clue what to make for dinner. There is one quiet window of time before the boys come home. Pete has made it back early, and we're hoping for a snatched ten-minute nap. But she's inconsolable for reasons she can't put into words, and I'm on my knees reaching for her.

I will always come, baby.

She's in my arms and slowly beginning the ritual of stroking my right arm. Her curls are warm and sweaty, and that dimpled cheek fits just under my chin.

I will always come.

I dance with her slowly—the rock and roll of motherhood—and I know this is a promise I can stake my life on.

I will always come.

When you forget your lunch. When you are sheep number five in the Christmas play. When you take up the recorder and squeak all the way through the Easter service. When you get that bad haircut. When you think you want to be a beauty queen. When you swear off fashion altogether. When you get lice.

I will come.

When the mean girls make you want to shrivel inside your skin. When a teacher intimidates you. When you intimidate the teachers. When you think you can sing and try out for a musical. When you get laughed at and people point fingers at your hair or your shoes or your too-bony or too-big hips.

My darling, I will come.

When that boy breaks your heart and you're stranded at college miles away. When the internship you thought was part of your calling falls through. When you get sick. When the car crashes. When you have more data surcharges than you thought possible. When you run out of gas, chocolate-chip cookies, and faith.

I will be there.

When you say your "I do," when you start your happily-ever-after, when none of it quite feels like you thought it would. When you don't know how to pick a mattress, when the sofa is in the wrong place, when you regret what feels like signing your life away to someone else. When you keep on keeping on. When you remember how to say sorry. When you need a safe place to say how cliché you feel all "barefoot and pregnant."

I will so be there.

When the baby won't sleep and the world's on fire with sleep exhaustion.

Sweetheart, I will come.

When your husband's out of work. When you're down to one car and have moved in with your in-laws. When your job threatens to break your heart. When toddlers make you question your sanity. When you realize that you've made the worst mistake a woman can make. When you've run out of tears and still the tears keeping coming.

I will come.

When you move and move and relocate again. When you pack boxes and dreams and hopes. When your life is a world of duct tape and questions.

I will still come.

When your home is warm and your heart is full. When you're at peace. When you need someone to share the joy, to watch the kids, to admire the dimples. When you want to remember that old recipe for mellctert, when you still can't pick a sofa, when you wish you'd never said yes to the dog.

I will come.

When you don't know where you're going. When you're the surest of yourself you've ever been. When you're holding on to faith with just your fingernails. When you're singing "Jesus loves me, this I know" and you mean it with every beautiful, miraculous part of your DNA.

Zoe, always I will come. One hundred different ways I will come when you call.

I will rock-and-roll you with my love and the promise that I will help you get back on your feet. I will hold your hand. I will rejoice. I will babysit. I will pass the tissues. I will wash the dishes.

I will come.

Tonight.

Tomorrow.

And the day after. And after.

And then the next one, too.

The Life-Saving Quirks of Our Kids

So this past summer one of those bad things happened. You know the ones that you dread but that you don't believe will actually happen.

This is the terrifying underbelly of being a parent. The vulnerable truth that your heart is always exposed and in the flash of a split second that tender organ can suddenly, shockingly, unexpectedly be pierced straight through with a fear that can bring you to your knees. You can anticipate it, you can try to prepare for it, but when it slams into you it's from such an unexpected angle that you don't even have time to spin around and look it in the eye.

We'd been on vacation for a week in the Smoky Mountains. Gatlinburg, Tennessee, is perched high up in a nest of peaks and trees that stand on their very tippy-toes, touching the sky. In the late afternoons the clouds settle in creamy swirls around those giants and you wish you had four-wheel drive to navigate the dangerous bends and curves that take you up, up, up to the cabins stitched into the side of those ancient hills.

We had twelve Bakers all living in a log house together, staying up too late and eating too many kettle-cooked chips. And it was just what you'd hope a family vacation would be: cousins and puzzles and brownies and front-porch rockers. We'd eaten and laughed and bruised our butts on the mountain ponies and coaster rides and ate the chocolate fudge and loved the wood carvers and retold all the old stories and adopted new family phrases (my boys can't stop telling everyone to have "chill vibes") and played our own baseball Home Run Derby at the local park and it was good. So very good.

But there was that one moment that kind of gut-punched us. It was so unexpected.

It happened in the middle of an amazing morning when the whole family went white-water rafting for the first time. We'd booked our trip down the Nantahala River weeks before. All twelve of us had our water shoes and sunscreen and excitement, ready to learn how to ride this river that runs through narrow gorges so steep that the sun makes its way down to the water only when it's directly overhead at noon. The Cherokee had named it the Nantahala, meaning "Land of the Noonday Sun."

It was a sticky hot morning when we arrived to meet our guides and be introduced to the river. Our kids were antsy bundles of anticipation as we sat through the instructional video and strapped on our life vests. Our river guide, Deb, vibrated with enthusiasm and we high-fived each other out of the sheer joy of getting to ride in her raft. But first each of our helmets and life vests were checked to be sure we were strapped in tight enough that a guide could grab us by our chest straps and haul us safely back on board if the Nantahala grabbed us into her unpredictable arms. We listened and emphasized for our kids the lessons in how not to whack a fellow rafter over the head with a paddle.

Then we were all loaded up into the bus that would take us upstream and drop us off at the Nantahala. It was organized chaos at the launch point, as dozens of rafting organizations from all over the state unloaded their guests and their giant red, yellow, or orange rafts from the roofs of their buses to wait in formation for their turn to launch into the river. You could straddle the state line between North Carolina and Tennessee right when you stepped off the bus. Jackson laughed when Pete told him he was in two places at once. Then Deb shepherded us into the long line of rafts waiting to launch. She kept up a running commentary of encouragement and instructions shouted over her shoulder as we hauled our raft bit by bit down the steep bank and finally, when it was our turn, into the river. Cool, dark, and brown green, the Nantahala welcomed us aboard. Deb asked us for a good name for our raft and we all laughed when Micah shouted out the totally underwhelming name of just "Jason!" And so it was that we slipped into the cool current riding Jason, the white-water raft.

I was in the middle row with Jackson next to me and my daughter behind me next to her aunt Kim. With giant, determined eyes, Micah had insisted that he would be up front next to his dad. He paddled with commitment every time Deb yelled, "Two forward!" And we laughed as Uncle Chris and Aunt Jill with Grandpa and Grandma and the cousins jostled us from their raft behind, trying to sneak by between splash attacks with their paddles. We were high on sunshine and the rolling delight of the river pulling us past high cliffs, with a sky so beautiful above us that it was hard to believe we weren't riding through a movie set.

Between the baby rapids and the big grandpa rapids, it was just exciting enough to be a tiny bit scary. Whoops and hollers splashed with us as we dipped and bucked through the white water, Micah and Peter leading the charge up front. My eyes were in the back of my head as I worried about my little girl staying locked in her seat, and I kept swiveling around to make sure her feet were locked into the plastic sides and seats the way Deb had taught us. I did not worry about my boys; I knew they were built for this kind of ride.

And then in the middle of a fantastic morning of beauty and excitement leaning into the curves of the river, Micah, my ten-and-a-half-year-old middle-born, flipped overboard right in the middle of a class IV rapid. I watched him arc high into the air and then disappear under the water. And I felt all the things you feel.

Noodle legs, limp arms, racing heart, the instinct to dive headfirst in after him, and the urge to scream at someone or start bawling hysterically all made it very, very hard to listen to Deb as she yelled out safety instructions. It was harder still to trust our guides to activate the rescue they'd been trained for.

They tell me that a whistle went off, that all the other rafts paddled into formation around my boy so that he couldn't be washed farther down the river, and that my brother-in-law and nephew in the nearest raft paddled hard and fast at him.

But I watched him go under the churning water again and everything moved in slow motion and it was all my worst fears in one endless moment.

But here's the weirdly quirky, wonderful thing in the middle of that terrifying minute: Micah is my kid who asks *all the questions*. In fact, just two days earlier I'd shared this about him on Facebook:

Some days I feel like this middle kid of mine starts every other sentence with the word "QUESTION!" (yes, just like Dwight Schrute). He's all information input all the time. One million questions a day and it's intense. And sometimes Jesus has to take the wheel, if you know what I mean. But man, his focused, fascinated brain makes for some amazing conversations. Anyone got one like this? Any tips?

Tons of moms replied, because it turns out lots of us are raising persistent, relentless question askers.

So he'd watched the pre-launch water-safety video and followed up with a million questions. Deb had patiently answered every single one of them. He had follow-up questions to his follow-up questions, and she answered those, too. He repeated the instructions about how to handle yourself if you fell overboard until we all knew them inside and out. He double- and triple-checked his own life vest. He wanted to know exactly what to do with your paddle in case of emergency. And as we boarded the raft, he leaned over with his lips to my ear and asked me in a quiet, vulnerable whisper, "Mom, if one of us falls in, will you be mad?" And I spun my head around to meet his eyes and stated as strongly as I could, "Of course not! Falling in would be an accident, and no one gets mad when accidents happen."

And then an hour later, he flipped over our heads and into the swirling, churning water . . . and he did *exactly* as he'd been taught.

His face, as it bobbed under the rapid and up above the water, was a picture of equal parts terror and focus. He floated on his back, legs straight out in front of him and pointed downstream, just as instructed. He kept hold of his paddle and used it to reach toward the nearest raft so they could pull him in. He stayed calm. He trusted the training and the answers, and they all came through for him.

He got dunked good and proper under some pretty scary water, but my insanely awesome kid and all his wild and wonderful questions paid off *one million percent.*

His uncle and cousin hauled him on board by his shoulder straps as we'd been taught to do. But there was a moment before he was safe when he was simply trying not to swallow the river. The raft rushed toward him, and the desperate rescue almost trapped him under that hulk of plastic. His body was under the raft, and his face was desperately trying to stay above water as the Nantahala kept coming and I kept watching him try to keep breathing under a face full of river. Remembering it weeks later still fills my eyes with tears and my soul with dread. But he believed he would be saved, because he'd listened to the how and he'd put into practice every detail to facilitate his own rescue. And he was indeed saved. As soon as he was pulled on board and our raft had come alongside him, he hauled himself from one to the other and into my arms. And we just stood there, with our life vests making it hard to get my arms all the way around him, wet and shaking but still breathing.

I think sometimes there's a temptation to overspiritualize big moments like these, so I'll simply say this: it always shocks me to discover that God actually does build into our kids exactly what they need. I believe with my whole heart that Micah was prepared in a way I'm not sure my other two were for coming through that experience with cool, calm actions.

And it's taken the edge off my irritation levels when it comes to the relentless questions. It's given me a new way to look at this habit of his. It's given me buckets of gratitude. And maybe there's another mom out there who can take some comfort in knowing that all those questions turned out to be my kid's life preserver that week. Mom, let your kids ask! Revel in those questions. Give your children your attention or give them Alexa so she can answer for hours, long after you've lost your energy and enthusiasm. But let's keep remembering that our kids are designed in unique and wonderful ways to meet unique futures that we can't possibly prepare for. But we can keep leaning into the gifts they have been given and finding new ways to multiply them.

Some mornings I still have to tell Micah I'm not ready to discuss the timelines of the demise of the dinosaurs before 7 a.m. But I don't resent the asking anymore. Because I remember. I remember his face as his brain fought wildly to find the answer to how not to drown in a rapid. And that information was a lifesaver. Literally. So I pull out of the driveway and take a deep breath and say, "Okay, what was that you were saying about extinction?" And I dig deep into my head to find answers for him. But what I'm really saying is, "I'm so glad God made you like this." And we turn with the bend in the road, and his questions stretch as far as the eye can see and I drive forward to meet them.

A Love Letter to Three of the Loudest Children I Know

*D*aughter, I want you to inherit freedom from me. The freedom to stretch your long awkward limbs, your mind, your appetite, your wonder at the world, and the gift of being a woman. So when you sit across from me, you know I am comfortable feeling full—of life and love and family and, yes, also food.

And sons, I want you to know that your mother loved being a woman and wooed you into how to make your wives feel loved. Not by what size they were or how they applied their makeup. But by how they weren't afraid to snort loud when they laughed. And said yes to the breadbasket when it was passed down the table alongside the soup. And no to the crowd when the crowd wanted her to do, say, or wear what wasn't her choice. And you were right there, holding her hand.

Because I know that you are listening to everything Dad and I do, love, choose, fail, and say. We feel you there, listening to us from across the kitchen countertop.

The active listening of children who are living sponges.

Children who don't so much sip the words that drip from their parents' lips but rather swallow and gulp them down with the skill of those accustomed to drinking from fire hoses. Especially on the nights I lose my temper and loose my wild tongue on a trail of collateral damage because really I'm just frayed thin around the edges and haven't paused to take care of myself today. So I slow down and practice self-care and the fine art of putting myself in a time-out until I can be trusted with my tongue.

But listen anyway, because I'm going to teach you how to apologize. I'm going to teach you the powerful tool of saying out loud when you are wrong and letting those words work their way into the heart of the person you hurt, so that healing can begin and you can be trusted to keep loving well. Every spoken word of relationship that spans a lifetime has deep roots in the soil of a thousand sorrys.

Watch me apologize, and then watch me be loved. Because I want to be a better teacher than the tomes of research and recycled opinions that say girls start hating their bodies young and that boys are simply victims of their own thoughts and what the sports franchises showcase as appropriate behavior.

Watch me, your mother.

I am going to dance with your father tonight.

Right here on the living room rug that is due for a good vacuuming, between the old sofas and the bookshelves that line our lives with memories of all the 101 places I've sat and read these pages 101 times.

Watch us as we write a new story.

See how dancing can look like doing the dishes together. And how passion can feel like opening your arms to the three kids who clamber into a family group hug. Or how your dad lies cramped up on that tiny sliver of the mattress to make room for a twelve-year-old with bad dreams. How he tells me as I huff and puff about "never enough room" that as long as his kids want to find comfort in his presence, he will keep folding back the comforter and inviting them in.

Look at us. Listen to us. It's okay. We do understand.

That passion is also much more than Dad remembering to take out the trash. Wildly right and ready passion is never embarrassed. I can tell you stories one day of how your father kissed me beneath the cherry blossoms and behind the fountain that sings beside the US Capitol until my toes curled. I can assure you that we keep the bedroom door locked some mornings not just so we can sleep in. But so that we can slip into the love song of bodies that have twenty years' worth of practice making the other person sing.

I know what it feels like to feel full. It is good. And I have memories of romance that could make a Hallmark movie blush.

I am not afraid of your crush or the days you're crushed by all the things you feel. Take my hand; I promise to hold on. Even on the days that means letting go.

Take lessons from your mother about the habit of making room for each other and embracing the space with generous love and the freedom to say how you really feel.

Don't shrink. Don't shrink back or away or out of your own convictions, body, life, dreams, or faith.

Hold tight, my darlings. Don't be afraid to keep growing bigger. Into a bigger view of the world and the remarkably, breathtakingly beautiful people who will weave in and out of your story and color wildly outside the lines of what you might have expected. Don't be afraid of them. People are people are people, and the person you're talking to there in the post office might be the most important conversation you have today. Don't miss it.

Keep pushing forward into the one exquisite life that has been given to you, and keep sharing it with the people around you. And we will pull up chairs around the old kitchen table with its surface graffitied with more days of paint and clay and markers than I can remember and we will unpack your days with you. And I will pop corn or pour Coke or coffee or put out trays of fudge or bowls of chips or maybe just an old journal or one night a bag of carrot sticks or Jackson's obligatory helping of Cheerios, and we will remember our story together.

Remember how your mother learned that Jesus loves me, this I know, for my children taught me so. And it creaked open her joy in loving others with the dirt-smudged hospitality of her grinning children. How *ministry* is often a misunderstood word and actually looks more like letting the neighbors come over to play than like publishing a book or standing behind a pulpit.

Welcome footprints on the front porch and down the hall. Shoes everywhere and stories shared. Big love that makes all the distance between us small and easy to cross.

Never stop taking first steps. And Dad and I, we promise to never stop believing in you when you fall down.

Part 4

Why the Middle of Your Living Room Matters

Our First Home After Fifteen Years of Marriage, Three Kids, and Nine Rentals

O n a hot Friday afternoon in June 2015, Peter and I signed our names approximately five million times and became first-time homeowners. We were both forty. By then we had lived in nine rental houses in three different countries and had three kids. And two years earlier I'd officially given up the dream of ever owning a home.

Until that Friday.

I cried when we got into the car after we left the title office. Then we stopped by 7-Eleven to get Slurpees, as one does to celebrate.

It had been more than seven years since we'd moved to Virginia. Before that we'd hopscotched between states and countries. We started out in South Bend, Indiana, as newlyweds for two years. Then came two years in Chicago, two and a half in Ukraine, two in South Africa, and then two in Michigan before we'd moved to Virginia, where our small rental house was supposed to be just a short-term plan. I hadn't even seen that rental in person before the day I pulled up at the curb and Peter showed us around the home he'd frantically found for his family after accepting a new position in DC.

That white rental house was frozen in time in the sixties (just ask the bright-blue bathtub and wooden toilet seat). The fake-brick facade in the kitchen was constantly falling off the walls, and the backyard was so overgrown with poison ivy and mosquito colonies that the boys couldn't use it the first year we lived there. When Zoe arrived, her bedroom was a closet.

But every summer when it came time to move, we couldn't afford it yet. And we'd promise ourselves just one more year of saving and paying down debt and then next June would be our June to move.

I would cry.

I would get really angry at my husband.

And eventually I would accept the unacceptable and try to figure out new ways to arrange the couches in a living room that didn't lend itself to easy configuration. Or room for more than five people at a time. We spent five years in that first Virginia rental before we could afford a slightly bigger rental in the same neighborhood. Seven years total renting in Springfield, Virginia. It was the longest we'd ever lived anywhere as a married couple.

But those first five years in the tiny white house on Joplin Street felt like an eternity. Five years in that awkward, compact place I was embarrassed to call home. Five long years.

Five years of waiting.

I wrote a lot about that house. I believe there are lessons I learned there still cemented between the bricks of that home. Even the faux bricks made of cheap reddish-brown plastic that were constantly popping off the kitchen walls. Interestingly, I mostly wrote about that rental as a series of guest posts for other blogger friends. I think this had something to do with how I allowed myself to be shamed by a house that seemed inadequate when I compared it to the lives and homes of the people around me. If I'm really honest, that house embarrassed me. And writing about it anywhere and everywhere other than at my own online home allowed me to distance myself from it.

I've heard from a lot of women who also struggle with feeling the same about their rentals. How we fight the feelings of inadequacy and frustration, of embarrassment and failure, which seem to attach themselves to the title of renter, especially when you're no longer in your twenties. I was a renter throughout my twenties and thirties and all the way up through three kids and into my forties. And walking that season with other women helped me feel less alone. I realized there are so very many of us who spend decades renting and who need one another's stories. And to remind one another that it is, in fact, a relief to be able to rely on someone else to fix the boiler or pay for the fence repairs or any number of other handy services that come with a landlord.

The thing is, I moved into that house feeling entitled to something better.

And I moved out of it five years later on a hot June weekend feeling like everything was a gift.

I had surrendered the dream of ever owning a home. Not out of a sense of a defeat but instead with the sense of relief that came from letting go of my own demands, my temper tantrums, my judgment of myself. When I let go of my shame—my sense of being defined by a lease, the inability to change out the seventies-style living room shades, or the fact that we were stuck with ratty carpet in our tiny dining area that my kids quickly destroyed—I stumbled into a welcome season of freedom.

I had spent a large chunk of those five years sometimes griping to, sometimes arguing with, and sometimes just sitting next to my idea of Jesus. I believed He was real enough and close enough to be there with me, sitting at the foot of our bed in the room I really never should have painted yellow. I prayed, and for me, sometimes praying is talking out loud, and I imagined a real human Jesus, who never owned a home of His own as far as we know, really listening. So much so that when I'd run out of complaints, I rested my head on His shoulder and remembered His words from centuries ago: "Foxes have dens and birds have nests, but the Son of Man has no place to lay his head" (Luke 9:58). That wise and revered Rabbi had nowhere to call home, no place with His name on the deed, and no expectation of it either. Instead, He invited us to make our home in Him. "Live in me. Make your home in me just as I do in you. In the same way that a branch can't bear grapes by itself but only by being joined to the vine, you can't bear fruit unless you are joined with me" (John 15:4, MSG).

Jesus offers us welcome and profound acceptance way beyond the state of our four walls or our carpets. And He promises to abide with us, if only we can take our eyes off ourselves for a moment to catch a glimpse of the glorious invitation to make our home in Him.

I'm not gonna pretend this is easy. It took me every one of those years as a renter to even begin to metabolize this truth. And it's not like I've arrived—I've just started letting go of the things I've felt entitled to, but it is such a relief, friend. Such a relief to invite people over whether I think my house is big enough or beautiful enough or any other kind of enough that causes me panic. We started just opening our front door anyway.

So that brings us to October 2014. We were living in our ninth rental just a few streets over from the tiny white Joplin Street house. It had more space and a sunroom that poured light into our lives. It was where we gathered with friends and over breakfast and for all the home-work and sticky art projects and trying to work our way through an Advent reading with minimal tantrums. And it's where I stopped being stressed by the pressure to own a home.

And that October after nearly two decades of being renters—the year I turned forty—Peter told me he thought it was time to explore buying a house.

At first I barely heard him. But he was sure. And then I didn't really believe him. But he was sure. So I held on to his own sense of sureness because I had grown roots where we were. I had made my peace with renting. I had dear friends who were close neighbors, and our kids were active in club sports and at the public school down the road, so moving wasn't on my agenda. I didn't need to own a home to feel at home in my skin anymore.

But Peter was hearing something from God, and I caught echoes of it in his quiet sure steps forward along the process of exploring home ownership. So I followed in his footsteps.

We met with a mortgage lender, a dear friend connected us with a real estate agent, and we slowly, cautiously explored what Pete was hear-ing to test if it really was perhaps the time for us to consider buying a home of our own.

We qualified for a loan.

Let's just say that this was a big deal for us, because we had arrived in Virginia seven years prior with debt in the six-figure range. Every spare cent during the past almost decade had gone into a black hole of paying off debt and bad financial decisions.

It had been a long journey.

Painful. And also deeply redemptive.

And then Peter's parents offered to help with the down payment, the bank gave us the green light and a pre-approval letter, and Peter spent months combing through all the listings. Houses would come and go in a period of days, and it was dizzying trying to keep up with it.

Where we lived in northern Virginia was crowded and very expensive. Peter caught a vision for moving us to Maryland, to a quiet corner of the country with less noise, less traffic, and less stress for him, with a commute into DC on a fast train instead of the throttled highways.

This move would also offer more space, more house, and more quiet for our money. We must have looked at more than a hundred houses online, and then nearly fifteen in person, driving the hour each way back and forth every time. And I still couldn't imagine that any of them would make moving worthwhile.

Then in March of the next year, Peter came into the room late one night to show me our house. We both knew it was ours the moment we saw it.

Down a quiet country lane on an acre of land, it had a vegetable garden, a playground, a koi pond, and a beautiful open-plan living area that felt like home the moment we laid eyes on it. Built by the hands of the couple who owned it, it was part of what had been a large farm, now divided into plots for the family, and it had twenty-eight birdhouses dotted along the property line.

We went to see it in the dead of winter. Even when it was blanketed in snow, we knew that it was home. We made an offer. And we prayed and we hoped and it was terrifying to hope. Because hoping is trusting God with the desires of your heart—and what happens if He doesn't grant them?

And then there was a miscommunication about updates the buyer would need to make to the septic system and a misunderstanding that resulted in a delay and finally a revised offer. And the day we submitted our revised offer was the same day another offer came in, much higher than ours. And although we'd written a letter sharing about our family and all our hopes and dreams for this home—a plea really—for a place to grow roots and raise our children and plant deep into the community, the answer came back, "No."

They went with the other offer.

I was sitting in a roomful of my best friends at one of our Tuesday-night meet-ups when Peter texted, "We didn't get it."

I was stunned. I was so stunned. I sat and cried and my friends didn't try to fix it. They just let me be sad without coming up with excuses for God. But I deeply needed to believe that this answer was from God and not from the whims of the universe. I needed to believe that when we pray and when we trust God with our hopes and when we ask Him to protect us from the decisions we don't know enough to avoid, He answers us.

Because He is a good God. And I believe this. And I needed to believe that the no was a loving act from Him and not just a matter of "Well, that's life." Because what is all this faith we talk about worth if in the moments of our greatest hurts or hopes it doesn't count?

So we prayed more and talked to friends and family who love us and we held on with admittedly very sad hands to the promise that He does, in fact, work all things together for good. For *His* good, which Peter and I believe translates into *our* good.

And then our entire family got sicker than we've ever been. I mean, it was ridiculous. It was a seventy-two-hour marathon of toilets and buckets and bowls, and the laundry running round the clock on repeat. One by one I watched each kid succumb until it was finally my turn. Pete was the last man standing, until he wasn't.

It was brutal.

We were shaken, and when my boys could finally straggle their way back to school, their faces spoke volumes about how relieved they were to be leaving behind what looked like the scene of a crime.

For weeks Peter had been emailing me links to alternate house options until I finally told him to stop. I sent him an email titled "I hate all other houses," and I meant it. I couldn't imagine another home that would meet Micah's passionate farmer's heart and his need for digging and planting and taking care of the land. Or Jackson's heart for wide-open spaces to play soccer and have Nerf gun wars. Or Zoe's delight in the purple bedroom that should have been hers. A house like that in our price range.

I just couldn't see a future beyond that house.

And I couldn't understand why God would bring us so close to it and then let it slip through our fingers due to a series of seemingly ridiculous misunderstandings and delays.

I prayed with other doubters before me for God to help my unbelief.

The first day after we had recovered enough from the great stomach-flu apocalypse of 2015, Zoe and I were headed out to tentatively pick up some food, when I got this text from our real estate agent: "Check your email! The other couple pulled out of the property! The agent is wondering if you guys want to resubmit your offer."

I pulled over in a library parking lot with shaking hands to text her back: "Oh my word! Yes! Yes! Yes! One hundred percent yes! How do we do it?"

It was stunningly unreal.

Peter was still sick from the night before. Lifting his head to read and process the messages and sign the contract was dizzying. But really, the whole process felt like that.

And when we got final confirmation that the house we had so hoped and prayed for was actually going to be ours, I was downstairs in the laundry room with Peter, and I cried so hard that I scared our kids when we came upstairs to tell them the good news.

I don't claim to know how God works. His mind is as vast as the universe He dreamed up and as deep as the oceans He poured out. But I do know beyond a shadow of a doubt now that God gave us this house. He made that abundantly clear. Everything begins and ends in His hands, His good hands that can be trusted to hold us as much when we mourn as when we rejoice.

So one Friday in June 2015 I stepped through the front door of the first house I have ever owned, and it was every bit as amazing as I ever could have imagined. I soon painted the front door a deep warm blue, and the first piece of furniture we moved in was a new eight-foot-long dining room table handmade of solid wood. It was so heavy that it took four people to move it. Seventeen years into our marriage and we finally owned a table bigger than the tiny starter table we'd told ourselves was temporary nearly two decades before.

While everyone else trooped back outside, I stood in the shaft of sunlight from the bay window with my hand gently stroking the top of that table, the place where hundreds of people would sit and gather and eat and share in the years to come, and I still couldn't believe it. Why are despair and sorrow so much more familiar, so much easier to accept from the hand of our God, than delight and celebration? Why does joy feel so undeserved and so nerve racking as we hold our breath, waiting for the hammer to come crashing down on everything we're too afraid to let ourselves love?

The kids unpacked stuffed animals and Nerf guns and dolls, and we ate unfamiliar pizza from a local joint on that table the first night.

And still I was afraid to exhale. I had become gifted at the apologetics of disappointment, so this was one of my first times finding words for the faith of prayers literally answered. I'm not sure what this says about me. Maybe it simply highlights my humanity, in all its weird and fragile experiences. But I'm colored by the stories of women all around me still living in their rentals, still waiting for their turn. I feel their ache so deeply that it's hard to imagine that it might be okay to step through this door and into this place where we're allowed to make nail holes in the walls with abandon.

As much as I had wondered how to make sense of losing the house, I struggled just as much with making sense of actually receiving it. Because that's how it felt: a gift to be received with open hands that had done absolutely nothing to deserve it. I looked down at the table and noticed the grooves between each of the hand-hewn planks and saw that crumbs were already starting to gather in the cracks. This beautiful new table would earn her keep in this house. This house that I didn't deserve.

What I understood was that the one way I could make sense of the gift was to make sure we shared it. So for the next three years, the table gained scratches and paint marks and Sharpie stains and a sandstorm of crumbs from a hundred meals hosted, friends invited over, kids crafting and making me crazy with their glitter glue. I just kept opening that blue front door and inviting people in—into the ordinary rhythm of our lives, into the contents of our fridge, with burgers and brats and hot dogs and corn and tacos and pasta in constant rotation.

Opening the door over and over again is an act of gratitude and a recognition that none of this is ours but rather it is simply an undeserved gift intended to be shared. And every time someone arrives and we get to offer them tea or Coke or water, I'm reminded how I was never entitled to any of this. But I sure get to enjoy sharing it. Zoe calls this little neighborhood we're part of our village, and it is quirky and so wildly warmhearted.

On the Fourth of July the patriarchs of our little street host a come-as-you-are, eat-all-you-can cookout that ends in fireworks. Sometimes at the corner house there's a night of praise and worship and a bonfire. On hot July afternoons the kids walk over to the neighbor's pool, and every other Tuesday night we keep opening the front door to our home group.

Laughter lives here. So does English tea with milk and plenty of sugar. And the four cats that sometimes make me crazy and sometimes are just the comfort we need. People come and go and I struggle to keep up with sweeping the wooden floors that are always covered in a layer of cat hair and dirt tracked in by soccer cleats. But every single night when I wipe down the last of the counters and fish crumbs out of the cracks in that dining room table, I pause at my bedroom door. I pause and let my eyes travel over the room that is the heart of our home, with kitchen, living, and dining all sharing one space. It physically hurts. All that gratitude pumping through my heart aches and as I turn off the last light, I know in my bones I am owed nothing. And I feel the challenge to give it all away. Every last nook and cranny and invitation and spot on our sagging sofa is multiplied if I can get over myself and remember to keep opening the door and giving this space away.

I walk down the hall to Peter, who's snoring already. I brush my teeth and my hair and slip into my softest old sweatpants. The window is open and the house sighs and I slide into bed and this is my prayer of thanksgiving. I receive this space not just with my hands but with my whole self, and I am grateful for the days the house is loud with people and grateful when it is quiet with alone time, and I am grateful that tomorrow we get to open the gift all over again.

Step Away from the Mugs

*W*hen I walked into a HomeGoods store last week, I stood there in my schlumpy jeans, my face still droopy after a healthy helping of novocaine and two shiny new fillings (one of the all-time *worst* things to have to spend money on), and nearly lost my ever-loving mind.

Because there on perfect display were row after row of gorgeous white mugs with an imperfectly organic finish. That is to say they were a little bumpy and not perfectly symmetrical, which added gallons of charm. Each mug had just one tiny word styled in gray slim text. They said "Coffee" and "Hot Cocoa" and "Chai" in a funky sort of typewriter wannabe font, and I wanted all of them. I wanted them forever and ever, and I *needed* them too.

I was overwhelmed by the compulsion to buy these fabulous fresh white beginnings with words on them that made me feel more stylish and more charming than I could ever be in real life. I mean, who even says *cocoa*? We always just say *hot chocolate,* and I don't like the taste of chai, but I really, really wanted cabinets full of those gorgeous statement mugs. And I swear I could hear Joanna Gaines whispering to me, "Go ahead, just do it."

Deep down I really want to be one of those people who has match-ing mugs. Matching mugs that you are proud to display behind glass cupboard doors or, even more daring, on open shelving! I stared at those spectacular-looking mugs, and I admit I held them in my hands and turned them over and fantasized about arranging them in my space and how every morning when I made coffee I'd look at them and they'd look back and tell me, "You've got this, you sensational, organized woman, you."

But the thing is, in order to make room for those mugs that I des-perately wanted to adopt, I'd have to trash all my existing mugs. And don't get me wrong—a *very* large part of me is tempted to do that daily. You see, there is nothing consistent about our mugs. They are a collec-tion of totally mismatched colors, shapes, and words, acquired thanks to years of Mother's Days, Father's Days, Christmases, and birthdays. Because if you present my kids with a mug that says any version of "You are the Best Mom" or "World's Greatest Dad," they will 100 per-cent buy it.

How do I know this? Because I have the eight mugs to prove it. Two of them are *exactly the same,* I kid you not. The same picture of a sad mermaid that says "World's Best Mom!" purchased two years in a row by my daughter at the school's attempt at fund-raising, a "Penguin Patch Christmas market," stocked with every single gift no parents in their right minds would ever want. The faux-crystal pink flower? No, thank you. The mega-diamond ring that will turn your finger green? Nope. The tiny guitar that you can strum at your desk? Please no. (I have all of them.) The mugs that have the words "Super Dad" or "World's Best Mom"? Every single time.

So in my cupboard, behind closed doors, I have an eclectic collec-tion of mugs that say the same thing. But while on the outside they read like precious sayings, what I hear in my head is, *We are NEVER falling for the Penguin Patch again.*

Sure, I say that, but this year while I valiantly tried to resist the tide of marketing and cherubic faces insisting they wanted my cash ("because I love you, Mama, and just want to get you something special"), I held firm. I replied that I'd *love* something special and that special things live at HomeGoods and I'd be happy to take the whole crew on Saturday so they could pick out individual gifts for their parents, who actually do need some new pretty dish towels or vases or oven mitts but who definitely do *not* need any more mugs.

But although my kids actually consented to this plan, what I did not count on was the sweet nature of the teachers at our school. And the awesome PTA that had—wait for it—set aside a special fund for kids who didn't bring any money to the market, so that no kid would have to go home without being given a chance to shop for a gift for their parents. Therefore, even when my rule-abiding daughter insisted to her teacher that she didn't need to buy anything because she'd been instructed by her mother that we were *not* getting anything from the Penguin Patch this year, she came home and told me tearfully that her teacher insisted that there was "no way your mom would be mad that you bought her a gift."

And, yes, my Scrooge heart melted when she told me that. But just a few seconds later it was plummeting as she whispered in delight into my ear what she'd picked out for me. Because girlfriend cannot keep a secret or a surprise. Yes, she'd bought me the exact same mug she got me last year, and there it sits now next to its sister and random assortment of cousins, and they all grin down at me when I open the cupboard and they remind me that my life is not something that can be whitewashed calm or controlled or perfect.

My life is exactly like that collection of mugs: all mismatched and so meaningful. And as much as I want to, there is no force on earth that could make me part with those stupid Mother's Day mugs I somehow get every Christmas, too. Trashing them would be trashing the best parts of who I am: these kids who love me with all the same enthusiasm and commitment this year as they did last year and who are desperate to put it into words and gifts that don't match but perfectly convey all their feelings.

So I pour my tea into that mug and try to give it the stink eye, but I catch my daughter watching me and when she asks me, yet again, if I like it, I grin so big. Because of course I do, baby. Of course I do. I love this mug that you picked out for me, paid for by a PTA that serves our public school with passion and compassion for kiddos who give their parents gifts in spite of what those parents deserve.

This is the stuff, man. This is the stuff that makes our cupboards and our shelves and our kitchens and our living rooms and our lives so stunning. Not the design, not the shape or the words or the color, but the undeserved glory that pours out of them. My mugs may not say "Cocoa" or "Coffee" or "Chai," but they sure do say "Beloved" and "Grateful" and "These are the Best Dang Kids Ever, Even on the Days You Totally Don't Deserve Them." Okay, I know that one is too long for a mug, so maybe I'll put it on a T-shirt instead. Until then it lives here in my heart alongside the memory of a little girl who picked out the same mug for me and a tiny ukulele for herself.

Because that's the beauty and the predictable surprise of life, isn't it? This ability to insist on our own way, our own plans, our own cupboards and then discover that someone was trying to give us a gift all along. And it won't look like we planned. But it will hold a hot cup of love that will warm our guts in the best ways.

So I stood next to that HomeGoods shelf of beautifully designed mugs and gently, reverently touched each one, and then I put them back and turned my cart toward the door and my real life with its janky, mixed-up mugs and the kids who gave them to me. Maybe one day I'll have a shelf full of flawless white mugs, but for now I'm the very best mom in the world, two years in a row! I have the mugs to prove it.

P.S. If you have a shelf full of gorgeous matching mugs, allow me to fangirl you and kindly resist any implication that I'm somehow judging you. Girlfriend, I want to *be* you. So go ye forth and revel in your mugs. Take pretty pictures of them for all the world to enjoy and then tag me on Instagram so I can aspire to that same shelf one day in the hopefully not-too-distant future!

P.P.S. For my forty-fourth birthday this year, a friend gave me *two* of those glorious white mugs. She'd heard all about my mug crush! I laughed so hard and with such joy that the people around us turned around to stare. And then I gave in to my dream and bought four more. I am now the proud owner of six, yes *six* (and I'm eyeing two more), beautiful matching white mugs with their funky font and words like "Bestie" and "Home" and "Crazy" (I avoided "Cocoa"), and I couldn't be happier. Just goes to show, our lives and our shelves have room for all kinds of new dreams. We get to keep saying yes to new ways to love the world around us as well as the world right here in our kitchens and beating in our chests and laughing in our middles. We don't have to be either kid-mug or grown-up-mug people. We can be *both/and* women.

Your Front Door
Is Your Superpower

*E*very other Tuesday night we open our front door, and grown-ups, kids, and the most eclectic collection of potluck dishes you've ever seen stream in. Some weeks I look forward to it. Some weeks I'm exhausted at the thought of it. But we just keep opening the door no matter how we feel. And three years into living in Maryland and opening our blue front door and wiping down the bathrooms and sweeping up the crumbs under the dining room table and vacuuming the rugs, I know in my homesick, aching heart that this is the single-most game-changing decision we've made when it comes to finding local friends.

What started on Tuesday nights has bled over into every other area of our lives. Into desperate, last-minute calls for someone to meet our kids at the bus stop when we're running late, to watch our girl while we're at hours of boys' sports practices, to help one another move, to celebrate career milestones together, and to carpool or meal train or help clear out that old garage. Endless, generous moments shared across families are like duct tape tying us always tighter and tighter together, all up in each other's business. And I can draw a direct line between that kind of closeness and the first time we opened our front door to a group of people who were pretty much still strangers to us and each other.

It started because our church was looking for folks willing to host a home group (in other words, a regular chance to connect with friends from church outside of church). Being total newbies to the area and to the church where we signed up, we stood awkwardly in the church lobby, wondering who else might sign up to join us. Maybe three couples did. And they invited other people. And the grapevine has continued to extend invitations and the group has multiplied and now we have more kids than adults and they run wild like in *Lord of the Flies* until the food is served. But seeing that most of them are seven-year-old girls, there's much more cooperation and way fewer injuries and a whole lot of talk about glitter and unicorns.

Our two boys help look out for the littles, which mainly means policing the trampoline and intervening when someone gets too enthusiastic about feeding the koi fish and comes really close to tripping herself and her dress and sparkly shoes into the water. Sometimes the boys offer everyone rides around the lawn in the wheelbarrow, sometimes they hide in their bedroom when the girlie shrieks of excitement get particularly shrill, but inevitably they're pulled off their iPads by their enthusiastic fan club.

Everyone troops in for dinner, although some nights the parents are lucky enough to feed themselves before the children remember that they're hungry and show up for their helpings. And when our youth pastor sits down on the window seat next to the mom of two of the girls in our group and they get out their guitars, everyone settles down in the lounge on sofas or the floor or laps and we do our best to sing (and sometimes we're even in tune!). But it all sounds like heaven to me. The tiny daughters lip-synch when they don't know or can't read the words, and my giant sons squish in on either side of their dad, singing with their eyes if they aren't singing with their words.

Recently, we started inviting folks to share a story or two about how or where they saw Jesus that week. We call them testimonies, but really they're just chances to tell us more about themselves and where they spotted God in their ordinary lives. We lean in and love to listen to these stories because no one ever gets too old for amazement. Getting to see faith through someone else's eyes is real-time encouragement and our kids love this part of the evening. And last week my little daughter, who still wonders out loud if this Jesus is something tangible or not, told me on Tuesday afternoon that she wanted to share a testimony. Then she practiced. And then later, after playtime and the potluck, she sat on her chair at the edge of the circle and quietly, seriously, shared about the God who cares about seven-year-old girls who struggle with that mean girl in their class who used to be one of their best friends. She shared how when we tell Jesus our fears and ask Him to help us, He actually does.

And then of course all the other kids had to share too. The adults watched and listened as their kids bore witness to a God who didn't just come to earth once but has made His home here among us. Who has befriended our children, who are learning how to spot Him by listening in on the lives of their parents.

Before long, a few hours on Tuesday nights every other week wasn't enough; we all wanted more. We had started our third year together by hosting a "state of the home group" night, which meant we ate more than usual because we'd brought in even more than usual and then we sat and chatted about what we'd loved about the past two years, what we wanted more of, and what we thought might be good new additions. We all agreed we wanted what happened on Tuesday nights to grow legs and walk out into the rest of the week with us. What still kind of catches me off guard is how naturally that happened.

First there was a group text and then a group chat and then before we knew it, the guys were getting together for "man time" to connect and we gals were hosting a women's event at church and gathering for our own weekend lunches and antiquing if we had the extra time. This grew into weekday dates and stolen conversations after church and dropping off meals at each other's houses and helping move boxes while always, always planning more and more playdates and sleepovers for our daughters.

The thing about building friendships means at some point someone will be standing in your kitchen on a day you wish you'd had time to brush your hair, put on real pants, or wash the dishes. It means at some point when you ask someone how she is, she will actually tell you. She'll tell you the unpretty truth and there will come a moment when you cross a line in the sand of politeness into a land where your conversations become real and not just conversational. This is both a good thing and an uncomfortable thing, and I can't recommend it enough.

Opening the front door is a revolutionary, boundary-breaking act these days. Welcoming people into your unfiltered life will be good for you. We keep doing it and are constantly surprised by how richly it multiplies anything we may have hoped for in the beginning.

Seven years ago I was writing about community online but didn't have any in my real life. Today I wouldn't trade these stories and faces and families and Tuesday nights and Thursday afternoons and Sunday mornings and family Thanksgivings and Secret Santa swaps for anything. It takes so little to open the door, and what comes in—what sneaks into your life—is the kind of wonder and miracle you can never actually expect until it's sitting on your sofa, eating your barbecued meatballs with a plastic fork while your kids constantly chime in to all the conversations. And you're full long before the meal is over.

Part 5

Why the Middle of Your Failures Matters

Why I Showed My Kids
My One-Star Book Reviews

ou don't get it, Mom. Kids can be cruel." It's what my eight-year-old son told me from the bathroom, where I was treating his head for lice. His eyes were red from all the crying after he saw his new buzz cut for the first time.

We'd shorn him. Because of the lice. I thought he looked handsome. But without all that thick hair, his eyes stood bleakly out in his face as he sat on the edge of the tub and told me how worried he was about being teased.

We're only halfway through being the new kids at a new school in a new neighborhood. And slowly we're making friends and settling in. But there's still the uncertainty that hangs around the edges. The big "But what will they say? What will they think of me?" The questions that hover around the edges of the school day or the baseball practice or Sunday school.

Maybe it has nothing to do with being new. Maybe those are the inevitable questions that come with the insecurity of being human. This worry about what other people will think. But the lice had to go, and we still weren't winning after three rounds of all the treatments and washing and purging.

So we buzzed Micah. All of it. He has thick gorgeous hair. We buzzed it all off at the kitchen counter and at first he was fine with it. He was fascinated by the falling hair and shook himself off like a shaggy dog when we were done. He was all for the change. Then he walked into the bathroom and looked at himself in the mirror.

I watched it happen. How his face collapsed and the tears started and his cheeks burned so bright with shock and embarrassment at what others might think. The change was more extreme, more noticeable than he was expecting. He slammed the door.

My heart ached for him. I offered to drive him in the morning so he didn't have to face all the curious faces first thing in the morning on the school bus. And he'd have a whole day of school under his belt before the bus ride home and its inevitable battering ram of fourth-grade opinions.

When he walked out the front door, he was wearing his hoodie. He was still wearing it when he walked back in again that afternoon.

His teacher liked his hair, he said. Her son had always wanted a buzz cut.

One girl liked it, and plenty of others told him it looked dumb. And as I stood there hugging him and rubbing his soft fuzzball scalp, I told him that was the thing about life—you will never have everyone like what you do or make or create or write or draw or buzz.

Like ever.

And then I took him and his brother into my little home-office nook and pulled up my Amazon book reviews. All the one-star reviews. He and his brother laughed nervously as I read them out loud, one by one. They hugged me and patted my arm and were so surprised when I laughed and told them it didn't matter.

"But why, Mom?"

"Because, sons, I like my books. I *love* them and I know that you guys love them and that Dad loves them. And I know that Jesus loves them, because He's the one who gave those stories to me. Those are the opinions that matter."

And I watched the idea dawn on Micah's face that maybe his opinion really was the most important one when it came to his own haircut.

It would be so much more convenient if everyone agreed with us all the time, wouldn't it? Convenient, less stressful, but likely not better. We need pushback and input and loving, tender feedback from the people who have our backs.

As for the rest of it, being human means there are going to be other humans who disagree or flat-out dislike the things we love, the things we stand for. You know what? They're allowed.

(Disagreeing, yes. Bullying, no. I'm talking here about the regular kid stuff, where insecure kids don't respond politely to changes in their peers. Bullying, well, that would be a completely different story. And thankfully that hasn't been the case when it comes to Micah's hair.)

But figuring out how we'll respond to people who disagree with us is such an important part of figuring out how to make sense of this world and our place in it. It doesn't have to change who we are. It doesn't have to make us go invisible. It doesn't have to make us hide our heads or our gifts. It simply means that they don't see the world the same way we do. Some are more graceless than others in how they point that out. Some have the tact of fourth graders.

But we still get to choose how we will respond.

Some days I choose laughter. Some days ice cream. Some days a hot bath and a binge marathon of my favorite shows. Some days I'm like Micah and I cry a lot first. But I'm learning to look myself in the mirror and recognize that that thing someone else doesn't like is something God gave me. So I write books not for the five-star reviews and not for the one-star reviews but because it's my way of opening and celebrating the gift I got from my Father God. Writing is like telling Him out loud, "I receive this gift and thank You for trusting it to me. I love it!" I write as an act of love, of gratitude, and of obedience.

On my best days I don't write for approval or validation; I write because it's what I've been given to do. I write as an act of unwrapping a gift. I write, and the fact that someone doesn't like what I write is simply proof that I showed up. I accepted the gift. I took the challenge. I made the art. I put myself out there. And the fact that some people don't like it or disagree with it is evidence that I made something in the first place.

"Congratulations!" I've been known to tell friends when they get their first one-star review. "You are now a writer who showed up with ideas in the world, and the world read them and the world reacted to them and that's proof that you shared them. You didn't hide your ideas and your stories and your art and your craft; you offered them back as gifts, just like they first arrived in you, and there will be plenty of people who are changed because of your gifts. So don't stop giving them."

Some days, I admit, I still wear a hoodie over my insecurity.

But on the best days, I forget completely what others think. I forget the hoodie and the awkwardness because I'm just doing the thing I've been given to do.

Like my kid—it's been days since he thought of his hair because he's too busy making plans for the next adventure. Too busy planning that snow fort, that perfect sled ride, that game of stuffed-animal tag. Until he captures a glimpse of himself in the mirror. And then . . . then I've seen him wink.

Financial Free Fall

*W*e were on a payment plan for years to pay off our first two kids. I remember with a kind of sickening post-traumatic stress the salmon-colored manila folder that traveled with us when we moved houses and states. It was fat from all the hospital bills it had eaten and that Pete and I were paying off, inch by painful inch. We joke often about how much those two boys cost us and how we got Zoe for a song, as she was the only one born when we had real medical insurance. The other two came on board while we had very tenuous self-bought insurance: once while we were living overseas and had only travel insurance, and once while Pete and I were both self-employed and had close to zero insurance between the two of us.

We had no idea how much having a baby could cost, especially when there were complications. We were grown-ups who took much longer than most to actually grow up in our financial planning and due diligence. We made decisions because we wanted to, not based on whether we could afford to or not. We walked away from high-paying jobs, moved overseas, and lived off our savings and Pete's academic-fellowship stipend, and we always blithely assumed that things would work out. For the most part they did, and that might have been part of the problem. Because you really can't keep moving countries and paying all the shipping expenses back and forth for your whole house to follow along behind you in a box and expect it to have no impact on your bottom line.

I'm making us sound like complete idiots. We weren't. But then again, maybe we were a little bit. Pete was much better at numbers than I was. I was oblivious, and it's taken me decades to dial in and understand our family finances. I sure wish I'd started earlier. It's the reason we're so rabid now about giving our kids a ground-floor understanding of the power of cash. It's why we make them save for whatever the latest, greatest toy is that they "need." They're welcome to earn the money for it through all the chores that a house constantly needs to keep chugging along. And if they can raise half the cash, we have committed to matching them the other half. So by ages seven, ten, and thirteen, my kids were already light years ahead of where I was in my twenties.

We leapfrogged from Boston to South Bend to Chicago to Kyiv to Pretoria and back to Owosso, Michigan. And when we arrived we were crippled by moving expenses, years without consistent income, and two babies who brought more joy and more debt into our lives than we ever could have predicted. I look back at our choices with a kind of compassionate awe, stunned that we could have been so foolish. So much so that when we couldn't afford to buy a house at the age all our friends were well settled into their beautiful homes and lives and careers, I looked around our living room and realized that the only ones to blame were ourselves.

Our Michigan years were a rebuilding of sorts. Of our marriage, our life hopes and plans, and our commitment to start paying attention to the details of being grown-ups, such as our credit-card statements. Pete got a job offer in Washington, DC, so we moved again—this time to Virginia—and settled into a tiny rental house with a backyard that could have doubled as a scene out of *Swamp Monsters,* so thick were the swarms of mosquitoes and poison ivy. This was the place where we would take out the manila folder to pore over how the payments were going and what was due when. Hospital administrators were kind and put us on as generous a payment plan as they could come up with. Pete and I both worked full time, and still the balances were slow to go down and the red statements in that folder were still as fat as ever.

The shame of those years still sticks to me some days if I let it. The shame and profound sense of failure. How could two college- and grad-school-educated individuals make such a fiasco of their budgeting? How could we have stumbled into credit-card payments that cannibalized our paychecks before we even got to planning out anything that went above and beyond the basics needed for day-to-day survival? We didn't flourish during that season—we survived.

It was so tense and so tight and so hard. The worst part was that we believed we deserved to feel every bit as bad as we felt, because who else was there to blame except ourselves? Debt and guilt are very heavy rocks to carry in the same backpack, so some days Pete and I took them out of our packs and threw them at each other. We'd go round after round of blame while the babies slept, and we hated how we ended up in this hole and tried standing on top of each other's heart to be the first to climb out.

Financial failure is a haunting, invisible crash and burn that no one wants to actually speak out loud, as the embarrassment makes your skin feel raw. So we worked and worked and worked and lost all hope that we'd ever actually be able to make a dent in the thick of all we owed. But sometimes the tides change so slowly that you don't even notice it at first. After full days of work and commuting and taking care of babies and cleaning up more projectile vomit than kids should really be capable of, I was slowly writing down the words that would become my first book. I am not a morning person; I despise being up before the sunrise. But for nearly a full year, I got up before my full-time job started and wrote from four to seven thirty in the corner of the tiny room that was stuffed full of toys—an area we loosely called the playroom. I wrote on the weekends and on holidays because I was driven by this crazed compulsion to write down our story. It became my first book, and the first advance payment was the reason we could finally begin to make progress through that manila folder.

That book set my story and our finances free, and slowly we could breathe a tiny bit in our budget. But still the shame was a cruel voice in my ear, and I couldn't shake the feeling that we deserved to feel terrible, because we'd done this thing to ourselves. It's a strange thing to hate yourself and blame yourself for the very thing that is drowning you. Like if you jumped into a swimming pool right after you tied yourself to a fifty-pound anchor, could you really justify feeling bad about the fact that you're drowning when you're the one who set the events into motion?

For years I believed we deserved our debt and our shame. And I believed we couldn't even go to God for sympathy or rescue, because who were we to ask for help from the dumpster fire we'd lit ourselves? So I steered clear of telling God how desperate we were, because I was too embarrassed to drag Him into our mess. I just kept telling myself that once we'd powered our way out, I'd be entitled to talk to Him about money again.

I feel so sad for that poor young mom drowning in debt and self-loathing, and I wish I could remind her that she'd never judge her own kids so harshly. If they dug a big old hole in the backyard and then promptly fell into it, she'd never stand at the edge criticizing them and demanding they figure their own way out before she could love them.

Nope, she would have been down there in the dirt with them a split second after they fell, holding out her own hands as the staircase for them to stand on to climb back out. Why on earth would our God, our maker, feel any different? Looking back I see that while I was trying not to cry all over Him with my shame and despair, He was there all along anyway. There He was with me at 4 a.m., pouring inspiration into my tired mind as I sat at my keyboard typing out that first book, trying to ignore the random toys that kept bursting into creepy songs or sound effects. There He was on the phone calls with the hospital finance folks. He was sitting beside me as I scrutinized what was in our manila folder and month by month marked down the payments we were making. He was with me when I crossed through the IOUs until we slowly made progress and the list of checked-off bills grew longer than those still demanding attention.

He was there when Peter got a job that came with great health insurance that made giving birth to Zoe so affordable that I actually cried with happiness this time during my pre-authorization conversation with the hospital employees. He was there leaning in through my friends who believed in my writing, through the agent who advocated for me, and through the publisher who said yes to me. He was there with Peter balancing kids as I was balancing writing deadlines, and then He was there in the driveway next to the trash cans the day I ripped open the envelope that had my advance check that would change so much of our desperate into our bearable. He would be there dancing and crying and celebrating with Peter and me. Because what parent wants to be left out of the sweet bits and the hard bits that make the sweet bits all the more gut-bustlingly meaningful?

No parent wants to miss that ride. No parent wants to watch from the bleachers when they could have been up close and personal, coaching and living and breathing and hoping and believing right in the very thick of the battle with the ones they love more than themselves.

Recently Pete and I wrote the final check to pay off my very last law-school student loan, seventeen years after we wrote the first one. Seventeen *years*. It's almost unfathomable. And before that we paid off all the shipping and moving expenses from years living between countries. And all the credit-card bills and hospital bills and what is this life where we're finally debt-free? We've long since given up the convenience of credit cards, and our kids always ask me at checkout, "That's a debit card you're using, right, Mom?" They're our miniature accountability partners, because they know what a big hole their parents had to climb out of and they're part of the program now as we all plan for the kind of family life we want to build together. One that helps even seven-year-olds make grown-up decisions when it comes to spending, because it took the grown-ups so long to learn it themselves.

The shame has mostly faded, but it's so familiar to me that I can easily step right back into how it felt. It was like a second skin for a long time. I know so many other women wear it for years without ever questioning where it came from. And if that's you, sister, I want to look you in the eyes and tell you what I learned and what I hope you learn much more quickly than I did: Love drives out shame. Love looks shame in the face, cups it with trustworthy hands, and won't look away until all that love has drowned out all that shame. Good fathers don't wait till their children have climbed out of dark scary holes before they decide to love them. Even if the kids have dug the holes themselves. Even if the kids were playing chicken at the edge of the holes. Even if the kids hurled themselves willingly into the holes.

No, sister, good God fathers come running and they don't pause until they've flung themselves into the deep heart of those dark holes to find their kids. To wipe their tears all smudged with dirt and shame. To hug them and light candles and bring the soup and the flashlights and floodlights and the safe steps out back to the surface. There are no holes too deep or too dark or too deliberate to keep the Father God out. He has been known to sacrifice Himself in order to get His kids out alive. We can trust that Father with our shame and our embarrassment and self-loathing and despair, and He will always offer up every single sacred bit of Himself in order to make us whole again.

How to Fail in Public

I recently bombed in front of a roomful of women I loved and admired. I mean, it was epic. It was the kind of bombing where your brain is literally yelling at you, "You are crashing and burning. Crashing and burning! Make it stop! Make it stop *now*!" Instead, you just keep talking, because the timer in front of you is still counting the minutes and you haven't used up even half of yours yet.

It was February in Arizona and I had been invited to speak at an event that was basically a Who's Who of women I had admired from a distance for years. But when they picked the speakers up from the hotel to take us over to the event venue, I panicked when I found myself sitting in the same minivan with them. Turns out I wasn't ready to make small talk in person with my heroes. So I tried to act normal and sipped my coffee as if I weren't freaking out on the inside or wishing I'd chosen the other pair of jeans.

They were kind and funny and warm and welcoming, and if all I had to do was spend time with them over coffee, I think I would have been okay. Instead, I had to teach. I had to teach *in front of them*. I was the very first in this lineup of speakers way more talented, experienced, and funny than I. As they all found seats in the front row to listen, I tried not to let my doubt and fear get louder than the lesson I had prepared. It did not work. I felt underprepared. Or maybe the problem was that I was overprepared and had too many words in my head and too many options for what to say, so none of it came out making any logical sense. Whatever the case, I had that experience where you float up above your body and start watching what's happening from the outside, as if you're watching a live-action car crash and can't look away. And you can't seem to make it stop; you can only keep going, wishing that help would come or that someone, somewhere, will take some kind of hope or scrap of new knowledge from what you're going through.

Just as I was starting to believe that maybe it wasn't going as badly on the outside as it felt on the inside, the giant screen with the ticking countdown clock in front of me crashed. Just seconds earlier the counter showed fifteen minutes clearly remaining in my talk. Then without warning it suddenly crashed to zero. I blinked, but I kept going, waiting for the techies backstage to realize what had happened and reset the stupid clock. But when they noticed, they must have assumed I'd simply run out of time. So they started up the clock again, only this time it showed a negative countdown, each minute a glaring, angry red accusation of running overtime.

I panicked. I stalled. I hoped that my missing minutes would be restored. But no, the angry red minus sign kept flashing, and after five minutes the words "STOP NOW" started flashing across the screen. And right in the middle of what should have been the climax of my lesson, I whimpered to a stop and walked off the stage. As I slunk back to my seat, one of my heroes leaned over from her chair, patted me on the knee, and said, "We've all been there." And then I died a thousand deaths in my red-velvet folding seat, by now the same color as my face.

The vice president of the organization I was there to serve gave me a shrug and a well-meaning smile. I sat burning up the oxygen around me, left to savor the acrid taste of my total bomb alone. That's how these things are experienced—in public but totally alone. I sat with my thousands of angry, hissing thoughts and tried to decide which one to listen to. The overwhelming majority of the voices in my head wanted to hightail it out of the conference center and back to my hotel room to climb into a hot bath and then into a fluffy towel, a giant pair of sweatpants, and bed. I wanted a humongous hamburger and hours alone to wallow in my shame and Netflix.

But there was one tiny voice that stood out above all the others. One strand of logic in my brain that told me that this was my one rare, valuable-as-South-African-gold chance to learn from some of my favorite mentors. I could choose to hide in my hotel room, or I could choose to learn from some of my heroes. I could binge-watch and eat, or I could shake off the failure and keep showing up to the next sessions to see how the greats did it. How they taught with humor and experience and grace and, yes, joy. That was what I really wanted—to be in the audience so all their giftedness could seep into my bones and I could carry their lessons instead of my failure out of the building with me.

It's never easy. We joke about learning lessons the hard way, and it's called that because it actually is hard. It's also awkward and uncomfortable and worth it. So I got up after my disastrous session and thanked people for their kind words. Then I found a seat in the audience where I could settle in for the rest of the weekend and practice the ministry of becoming a student again and offering my amens and encouragement to the women on the stage doing what is a very difficult thing to do: helping people learn without them even being aware of it.

I loved it. And I hated it. It was hard to know that I was the weakest link in a weekend of learning. But it was good to have that lesson metabolized by my very bones—what I would do differently next time and the even more important revelation that failure does not, in fact, kill us. That we're capable of showing up again the very next hour with our faces intact and our smiles open and our hands filled with a notepad and pen and a willingness to go learn how to do it better next time.

I have a friend who tells me that God will always humble us, either in public or in private. (And we laugh together because if the choice were up to us, private is definitely preferable.) She's taught me that when your profile photo on the book cover or signage is not the right/most flattering version or your name is spelled wrong or your biography experiences are confused with someone else's, you should just grin and thank the good Lord for that dose of private humbling. Lest you fail to learn your lesson and He upgrades the education to one with a public audience. I learned my lesson that day in public but also in private because I was the only one who truly understood the gist of how hard I'd fallen. Because I'm the only one who really knew how much better that talk could have been. And I (grudgingly) thanked God for taking the time to humble me and give me the gift of getting to be in the audience, learning from women who've failed and learned and tried again for years longer than I've been alive.

My kindest teachers have resisted the temptation to rub my failures in my face. They have simply passed me a cup of iced coffee and offered the kindness of saying very little, of refusing to pity me, and instead just helping me get up off my behind, never doubting that I would, and then giving me another chance.

Each new chance is another opportunity to fail. But more than that, it's a chance to apply what we've learned about failure. And it's a gift. Because one day the people behind us will fail too, and we'll remember what it felt like and pass them the iced coffee and the tender smile so they'll be brave enough to get up off the floor and try again too.

Part 6

Why the Middle of All Those Sports Practices Matters

When Our Kids Have "Unrealistic" Dreams

*W*e rode home in the dark from his first tryout for track. He's followed the career of Olympian sprinter Usain Bolt for years now. He talks about the Olympics as if it's a real date on his calendar in the future. And I hold on to the steering wheel, unsure how to put into words all the thoughts I'm having. Thoughts about caution. About realistic dreams. About how gold medals are not the gold standard for accomplishment.

But his eyes are lit up by the streetlamps that flash past us, and I know that he's way out ahead of me already. Do I really want to be the anchor here holding him back? How do I cheer for him while also being a plumb line for truth? How do I let him know that just because we wish something doesn't actually mean it will come true? That just because we run our hearts and lungs and guts out does not mean we'll end up winning?

What then?

What of small boys with big hearts? What of fierce boys who still can't make their legs grow longer no matter how hard they wish it.

What do their mothers tell them?

When they ask you if you believe that they'll make their way to the Olympics someday, what do you—that mother behind the steering wheel who can't see the future—tell your son?

We pull into McDonald's for ice cream because two decades ago my own mother used to remind me before every race, "My darling, if you win today, I'll buy you an ice cream. And if you don't win, I'll buy you *two* ice creams!"

He knows the promise by heart.

I heard him whisper it as a reminder to me on the track as all the kids from his age group gathered around the coach. All these giant kids. How did they get so tall? And his blond hair bobbed at least two inches below them, his smile always ready for any sign of welcome. His ability to blend into any melting pot is gold-medal standard.

It was so cold standing out there behind the chain-link fence watching them come hurtling down in packs of hopes and dreams—all those boys with their faces set into the wind and their arms pumping. I was that weird mom cheering every heat home. Because when last did I hurl myself down the track with such desperate commitment? When last did I go for it with everything I had, knowing I might come in last?

He didn't though.

He didn't finish last.

But he didn't finish first, either.

We sit in the dark car and he eats an Oreo McFlurry and I try so hard to find the words to show him that this faith we believe in is about more than gold medals. But I don't want it to sound like a cop-out. I don't want it sound like an excuse. I don't want to be the mom he told me I was last week who "doesn't seem to really believe me when I tell you I'm going to the Olympics."

I want to be the mom who believes all things and hopes all things.

So I tell him that. In a McDonald's parking lot over ice cream and dreams, I tell him that I want to be the mom who believes in him. But I don't leave it there. I tell him, "Jackson, I also want to be the mom you can count on to tell you the truth. And often in life there are things we wish for, things we desperately want, that we won't get. But that doesn't mean we give up before we've even tried. Before we've even started fighting for it.

"I believe that you can fight for these dreams, Jackson. I will believe that you've got the fight in you, so I will help you. I will be the mom who sees every practice, every time trial, every lap as the fight you are winning. That's the gold medal of showing up—doing the hard work when no one is looking. That, son, is the stuff of medals."

I'm not sure he believes me, although he nods. He tells me that is good advice.

As I turn down Rouse Parkway, I tell him that I will always show up with him. I will always cheer for him. I will always follow through by putting him on the path headed to the goal he dreams about. I will race with him.

We might not always win.

But no one will be able to say we didn't run our guts out on the track, even when no one was really looking.

"I'll be looking," I tell him.

I'll always be looking.

I don't want to preach to him; I want to live with him. But I do tell him that quirky thing about Jesus—how anytime He did something miraculous, He was always trying to get people not to tell anyone about it. Upside-down Jesus.

We drive home in the dark and I leave him with that image. Jesus, who didn't need medals or praise to feel like He had been great at something. That sometimes greatness is taking the time before the race starts to help the kid who had his number pinned upside down.

He nods.

Sometimes gold medals are given in the dark.

What Happens When You Lose

*I*t's one thing to see your newborn cry. It's the only way they know to communicate. Crying, farting, burping—that's about it. Until they hit eight weeks and finally figure out how to smile, thereby keeping their exhausted parents fawning all over them, despite the fact that it's been an eternity since anyone has slept more than three consecutive hours.

But to see your middle schooler cry? To see your nearly teenage son weep his guts out? That's terrible. That's something so desperate you aren't prepared to handle it, and you might end up calling your husband in a panic and putting him on speaker phone because you need help right now this second and someone has to fix it. Because there's no way your twelve-year-old should be sitting in the car next to you with tears burning down his cheeks as he holds his face in both hands and lets the sorrow and disappointment just stream out of him.

Just remembering it makes me want to throw up.

We were new to the school. New and feeling out of place. The one homing beacon in a totally new environment was soccer. Soccer was and is my oldest's safe place. He has the body of a natural athlete. He's like a dancer or a gymnast with a firecracker attached to his heels—all lithe muscle, disciplined and controlled and fast. Honed to push himself for hours. What he lacks in height he makes up for in speed and determination. Every summer for three years, he's spent eight hours a day, five days a week, at soccer camp. Hours of drills and running the same plays over and over until he had an actual six-pack to make my husband jealous.

That's Jackson. Furiously determined and utterly confident in his ability on the soccer field. While everything else was new in sixth grade, soccer was still home. The middle school was hosting tryouts every afternoon for the first two weeks of school for their two teams: A and B. We'd been to their summer training in the evenings where we knew no one. We had him show up on hot summer nights to try to put him at ease with the new players and the unknown coaches so that when tryouts arrived, he wouldn't get in his own way. We didn't want him to let his head talk him out of what we knew he knew his legs could do.

Tons of kids showed up after school. It was competitive. And all he wanted was to make a team—any team.

Despite the school's being a good forty-minute drive from our house, we'd chosen it as the best fit for middle school, and one of the big reasons was soccer. We knew that it would feed his passion for the game and also create room for organic new friendships in a school where pretty much everyone else had known each other since kindergarten. So he showed up to tryouts in the Ronaldo shirt and shorts he'd gotten for Christmas and we watched him find his way. We watched him start conversations with new friends and figure out the style of the coach. But mostly we watched him play his guts out. From first whistle till last. Peter and I took turns hustling over after work through gridlock rush hour to get there before tryouts were done so we could catch him in action.

This is the part where I am unashamed at our pride in our kid and how hard he worked those weeks of tryouts. How he juggled so much more homework than we were used to with new schedules and long afternoons on the soccer pitch and came home to figure out new technology to turn in his new homework.

We were fueled by his joy. His joy at this opportunity and this game he loved. And slowly the circles of old friends opened to let him in on the soccer field and then in the classroom. He let his playing do the talking, and soon the other players were talking about this sixth grader they thought would make the A team. Hope is a terribly dangerous thing, isn't it? This hope that started to grow in him to make the first team with the eighth-grade guys who'd taken him under their wings like a kind of newbie mascot.

So we'd pick him up and hear the laughter of new friendship, and our hearts told us yes. Yes, this was all worth it. All the driving and training and more driving because our son was finding his way into friendship and a sense of purpose in his sports, with a coach who seemed just as interested in the character of his players as their abilities.

Then on the Friday before teams were going to be announced on the following Monday, three of the sixth-grade boys were pulled aside and told they'd made the A team. Jackson was one of them. And our son came flying off the field and didn't touch the ground once. When he got home with his dad, he flew right into my arms and the middle schooler was both my baby and this man he was growing into. My firstborn, my Jackson Jo, who is named after me, was so proud of how his hard work had been recognized and earned him a spot on the first team. It was like watching him becoming a man right there in front of me in the living room. I didn't know that this kind of parenting existed. The kind where you're watching them take more than first steps down the hall. Where you're watching them take big steps into their own lives, becoming the people they're meant to be. And it hurts your insides because the love is so big, it pushes up through your heart and explodes across your face.

Friday we were flying high.

Monday we crashed hard.

Saturday there was a scrimmage that was compulsory to finalizing the A and B team lineup. Except we didn't know that. We thought it was just a pickup game. For fun. So although our kid begged us to take him—insisted he had to be there—we said no. It was my birthday weekend, his brother had his first football scrimmage, we were hosting a massive church cookout at our house, and we didn't have the capacity for one more commitment. Not when we thought it was take it or leave it.

So he let it go, our boy. He accepted our answer and moved on. And we didn't think about it again.

Until Monday afternoon.

I know it is bad before practice is even over. He is practicing with the B team. A great group of guys, but not what he'd expected. Not what he'd been told. And I can tell by the sag of his shoulders and the spark that has left his footwork that something went wrong. I sit on the concrete steps leading down to the pitch and feel the wretched knot grow tighter and tighter in my stomach. It is hard to swallow. I feel frozen in time under the hot September sun, and at the last whistle I don't know if I should approach him and his coach or wait to hear what he says.

Because I battle against my tendency to want to helicopter, I clench my fists and keep my seat and tell myself, *It's okay. He's growing up and learning to handle his own business.* But we walk to the car in total silence. I open the back door of the minivan and he slings his bags in and then pulls himself into the front seat, eyes staring straight ahead.

I start the engine and head out of the parking lot.

"Hey, bud, you okay?"

He looks straight ahead out the window. I can see that his eyes are unfocused. He swallows.

"No," he says. "I'm on the B team."

I'm so confused. Not because the B team is less than but because it's not what the coach had said three days earlier.

"What happened?" I ask. "Help me understand, bud."

"It was the Saturday practice," he says. "Coach said I was supposed to be there so they could confirm their final decision. Because I didn't bother to show up, they decided to play me on B."

Then he turns to look at me.

"I told you, Mom. I *told* you."

Then he starts to sob.

Not a soft cry. A soul-wracking sob. His whole body heaves. I'm on the highway by now and can't comfort him. I can't wrap my arms around him. I can't hold him and I can't take all that pain away from him. I can only watch him in a stunned stupor and keep my eyes flicking between the traffic and him. My devastated, precious son. He cries so hard I'm afraid. I call his dad and put him on speaker, but Pete can't make any progress because Jackson is crying too hard to hear the words of encouragement.

I drive in a daze.

My son weeps.

There aren't words.

It wouldn't help to say that this is "just" a game. "Just" a sport.

It wouldn't help to say that the B team is a great team. It wouldn't help to point out that many guys didn't make any team at all.

Because my son is sitting next to me, stuttering out between sobs how when he arrived at practice today and walked over to where the A team was gathering, as his friends looked up to high-five him, the coach called out in front of everyone, "Nope, you're with the B team." And then, with everyone watching, he had to walk himself to the far side of the field and shake his head when the guys there all asked for an explanation. Because he didn't have one.

We arrive home and I'm still so confused, yet my boy has calmed down now. The dirt on his face is smudged with muddy trails left by his hot tears. But by the time I've made him sweet tea and popcorn, by the time he's eaten half of it, by the time I've doubted all our choices, he's telling me that the B team is fine. The B team was what he'd hoped for in the beginning. He's just so confused because what did he do wrong? And I want to get down on my knees and take his face in my hands and say what his dad tells him later that night: "Jackson, if for even a second we'd thought that scrimmage was mandatory, we would have made it happen to get you there, son."

He believes us. He says he believes us and that he's okay.

I'm not okay.

I debate for hours whether or not I should reach out to his coach. I'm a newbie mom of a brand-new middle schooler and feel utterly out of my league. But an older, wiser mom friend advises us to go ahead and just ask what we missed and what we misunderstood so that we can try to connect the dots for our kid.

So I do. Late at night I write several drafts before I've crafted a calm-enough email explaining our confusion that a kid could be bumped from a team because of missing a pickup scrimmage. And the next day his coach skips the email step and calls me directly, and it turns out that being the grown-up was worth it. It's worth it to ask awkward questions so that you can figure out the facts. It's worth it to talk calmly in person, one adult to another. This is not being a helicopter parent; this is being a grown-up, which most of the time I forget that I am. Most of the time I feel like the kid waiting outside the principal's office. But I get on the phone with Jackson's coach and finally figure out what happened.

Our conversation uncovers the fact that our email address had been mistyped during the transfer onto his group distribution list. So we never got those final instructions that went to the group about the mandatory scrimmage. And we never got the follow-up email announcing the team lineups. So our kid showed up unaware to practice that Monday and got sucker punched. Because if there's one thing that we grownups owe our kids, it's the ability to trust our word.

And since Jackson's coach is the radically trustworthy man we now know him to be, he was horrified to hear about all the miscommunication. He apologized and then said the words I would repeat to my son verbatim: "Your son's character is what impressed us at practice today. We always knew he was a talented player, but this team is about more than that. And the fact that he brought his A game to practice even when he was so disappointed and so confused just confirms what my other coaches and I were already talking about before you called. Your son has earned his place on the A team. You can tell him that I expect to see him on the A-team field tomorrow."

I actually wrote it down word for word. My hands were shaking, and I went to find my boy. He was excited. Sure he was. But there was something else I saw there behind his glasses. I saw the face of a young man who was just relieved he got to play at all. Who had faced his first real loss and discovered that you can't lose what you love. You just keep chasing after it and you will find that the joy of it never leaves your bones. A team or B team, you play because you love to play. Not because of what other people say about how you play.

Suddenly A team had lost a lot of its glitter and it had become about soccer again, which of course is really about life. We play to see who we become through the playing. Not for medals or applause. We play because the playing says something about who we are.

But this story still hurts.

I think it hurts me more than it hurts him. That sense of having let your kid down without even realizing it.

But I watch him play now with that team of kids who have become some of his best friends and I know they're not just playing together; they're growing up together.

At the end of the season, each boy got a medal with his name on it and the verse that has been the heart of their season together: "They collapse and fall, but we rise and stand firm" (Psalm 20:8, CSB). Jackson has quoted it to us this year more times than I can count.

Challenged by homework? Frustrated on the sports field? He always talks himself around to this reminder: "But we rise and stand firm." And when we're driving home the forty minutes one afternoon long after the season has ended, I tell him about how my day got kind of weird and sad in the middle and he interrupts with, "Dang, Mom, that really punched you in the face, didn't it?" I'm so startled by his take on it that I can't help but laugh.

But he knows what that kind of punch feels like. "I know what you need, Mom," he says while reaching for my phone to put on a song. "I got you. I got you, Mom. Just listen to these words, Mom."

I'm driving and he's DJing and we're both car dancing and singing at the top of our crazy guts about what home feels like, and the sunshine spills across his face and reflects in his glasses all the love I feel stuck here under my rib cage.

He's not my baby anymore.

Gladiators

*I*feel as though I've been playing football with my second son since the day he arrived in this world in a fury of push and pull and tug and tackle. His birth left me with bruises and scars, and to this day we butt heads and hearts on the regular. He was born with a massive skull, and now at ten years old, his body has finally caught up. It's as if football came woven into his DNA, beating around his heart with all its pent-up passion for pushing hard at the world around him.

He is a force of nature. His dad and I will wake up on a Saturday morning with no plans other than to maybe fold the laundry and lounge around watching Netflix in sweatpants. But instead we'll often find ourselves halfway to the pet store or the gardening shed or mixing up a batch of fluffy slime or waist deep in water, cleaning the fish ponds before we stop to ask, "But how did we get here? This was never the Saturday plan."

But Micah. His drive can reroute the entire family, and we'll be miles down the road before we look at each other and ask again, "How did he *do* this?" He has the drive of a running back and the immovability of a linebacker and there is no resisting the force that pours out of him as he steers us toward his goals.

I've often muttered to his dad, "I sure hope the girl he falls in love with loves him back, or we're all in trouble." Because this kid latches on to something like a heat-seeking missile, and there's no altering his course.

So of course he's been battering at his dad and me for two years now to allow him to play football, and we resisted. We persisted in citing stats and studies for protecting the heads of young boys and made him wait till he was nearly ten and weighed more than his older brother. For two years he has marched toward this single destination: full-contact football. And for two years he's had this mantra on repeat: "Football is my favorite sport." Without ever having set foot on a field. He had convinced himself that this was his game.

I wondered what the reality check would be like after his initial practice. It was August, brutally hot, when he suited up for the first time. Like a scene from *Gladiator,* he stepped into his armor: pads and helmet and mouth guard and cleats. He wore his dad's number 55 practice jersey from high school and it fit. It fit our fourth grader. He wore it like it was always his, and by the time he stepped onto the practice field, he was one of the few kids already familiar with the ins and outs of strapping on pads and snapping on headgear and quick to help his future teammates. I sat at the sidelines of a field that hadn't been mowed most of the summer and the grass itched my ankles.

Somehow I didn't realize that practice would involve all that gear. I felt the sun start to scald the back of my neck and I could see even from half a field away that Micah's face was turning the brick red of his Dutch blood. But still he ran. He ran and ran, lap after lap, always leading the pack. Practice after practice, the coaches began to teach the fundamentals of this blood sport to a pack of hungry young men. I watched in amazement as they graduated to turf and two-hour practice after two-hour practice, night after night, five nights a week. My son stepped into the words he'd spoken two years before and made them true.

This is his game. This is where all his bulk fits in a way that sometimes it doesn't in the classroom next to kids half his size. On the football field he could stop holding his oversized limbs in check and let them loose to run over, under, around other players. He welcomed with grim glee each hit as a defender slammed into him and he didn't let go his dogged grip on the ball.

I watched with big eyes and a mama's heart and an immigrant's amazement at this sport so foreign to me. I've often thought of professional football as an insanely overblown kind of idol worship. I couldn't understand the paychecks or the feverish commitment of the fans, and I definitely couldn't relate to the stories of parents who obsessed over peewee games and devolved into hand-to-hand combat over a bad call or screamed bloodthirsty threats at the opposing team of nine- and ten-year-olds. It was utterly bizarre to me. You know where this is going though, yes?

His first real game was on perfectly manicured, painted, prepared turf, wrapped around with stadium seating that put to shame all those soccer field practices with parents sitting on the ground or camping chairs if we remembered them. I was already out of my league in the stands, when a version of myself I've never met before entered my body. Mostly ignorant of all the rules of the game, I at least understood the fundamentals: if you're a running back, get the ball and run as if the very hounds of hell are chasing you, and then keep running until you cross the finish line at the end zone.

Pete and I weren't sure if Micah quite understood all the concepts of the game plays yet. But running like a steam engine as hard and fast and far as you can with the ball? His brain had latched on to that and made it his own. So on the Saturday morning of my birthday we were in the stands at the edge of bright-green turf, screaming till we were hoarse as our football junkie got his first real high of a game he'd dreamed about for years.

It wasn't a pretty game. It was an early scrimmage to give two green teams a chance to put the idea of football into practice. Most of the game was stop go, stop go, start again, with coaches on the field and in the ears of their players, encouraging, correcting, urging them forward toward the end zone. But it was slow going, boys running a few yards at a time and doing their best to block with their miniature man bodies. So many kids like our Micah were so new to the game, all still finding their way. We had settled into the comfortable rhythm of fits-and-starts football, when it happened. Somewhere in the second half, on an un-suspecting play, the ball hit Micah's hands and the way opened up ahead of him and we were all stunned to watch him take off on a fifty-yard dash with wide-open field ahead of him.

As he took off for the end zone I entered an out-of-body experience. On the third row from the top, I was on my feet, arms windmilling in the direction of the goalposts, screaming as if his life depended on it. "Go, boy, go!" I yelled. "Run, son, run, run, run!" I screamed as my fingers pointed in the direction of victory, arms swinging like an air traffic controller, and felt the stupid tears clogging my voice. And I needed my voice because I'd entered that phase of sports-momming when I was convinced that my voice and my voice alone was going to carry my son into that end zone.

I yelled and he ran, a blur of green streaming across the turf as defenders grabbed hold of him and he plowed on anyway. Relentless, my tank of a son. He ran fifty yards for the only touchdown of the game, and I felt as though I'd run each one of them with him; my heart was pounding and my breath came in ragged, raging gulps. He had steamrolled his way down the field, and his team celebrated their one moment of victory in a game they lost, and I was just 100 percent hooked.

Every Saturday, crushing heat or pouring rain, we showed up to bear witness as two rows of tiny gladiators faced each other and fought another battle that had their parents on their feet stamping and cheering. After a strong start, they started losing, game after game. And still they practiced two hours a night between school and homework, learning football play after football play. And Micah told me their secret, their never-giving-up, holding-on-to-your-grit-with-both-hands kind of secret: "We're not teammates, Mom. We're brothers."

And he showed up for his brothers and took hit after hit, and I made sure to meet with his teacher to explain the bruises on his forearms, his sides, his legs. His dad scoured Amazon and bought the best kind of arm pads we could find. And never once did his enthusiasm waver. Not when they played in temperatures pushing the hundreds. Not when they lost game after game. Not when his youth pastor came to cheer and ended up watching him lose. He kept showing up for his team and he was the first on the field and the last off.

Finally there was a game when they were up again. And then tied and then up again and then tied. And then it went into overtime. And double overtime. And I had bitten the insides of my cheeks raw.

Our boy got the ball and made the play that would have won them the game if he hadn't given in to the team's good-natured begging to spike the ball in a victory dance if he pushed through the defenses into the end zone. So he made the game-winning play and then made the victory dance that cost them a penalty. These miniature warriors were so confused about why they were lining up again for another play instead of celebrating a win. Afterward my son would tell me he was shaking so badly with the fear of becoming the reason that victory slipped out of their hands, that he could barely stand upright on the field. That the referee had to come over and put a hand on his back and tell him, "It's okay, son. You still have a chance. You're still in this." And they were, and they blocked their opponents' attempt at a conversion and got their first win by the literal skin of their teeth.

It's the strangest thing to be stunned by your kid's courage one minute and want to take him in your arms to rock and comfort him the next like you did when he still smelled brand new. Every game I ran the whole gamut of parenting emotions and found myself falling in love with this new side of my stubbornly fantastic kid. And then the wildest thing happened: they made their league playoffs by the craziest of flukes. The undefeated team in their league chose to accept an invitation to play up a league for the championships, so that left our boys entering a playoff tournament they never expected to join.

Micah accepted this development the way he does all things that he sets his mind to: with a "but of course" attitude that expects what he believes to be willed into existence. So to my great horror I discovered that the championship game we never expected them to play in was suddenly on the calendar. The same calendar that had months ago booked me out of town at a speaking event. So I boarded a plane as my son strapped on his battle gear, and while I was teaching he was turning all his single-minded determination on this singular goal. While I was facing my fears, my kiddo was also going to battle.

After my event ended, I sat on the curb outside a Chili's restaurant before going to the airport and called Pete, who recapped each play. My academic husband spoke with emotion crowding into his words and tears crowding into his throat as he described the courage of a team of nine- and ten-year-old boys. I sat on the pavement and relived the game, play by play, through my husband's eyes.

How they had played a team they had lost to twice already. How Micah broke through tackles early in the game to earn a first down. And then again. And then just before halftime, fifteen yards from the end zone, he ran into a wall of boys, spun loose from their grasp, and darted through a hole for the first touchdown of the game.

Peter was a line judge watching it all unfold from the field, and our eldest, Jackson, couldn't contain his excitement and came down to the field so he could hug his dad in between plays as they both kept their eyes on their brother and son. In the second half, momentum swung to the other team and they scored. But a failed conversion left Micah's team with a one-point lead.

Then midway through the final quarter, Micah's team took possession of the ball "deep in their own territory," as they say, and it put them at serious risk of giving their opponents an easy touchdown. The other team smelled opportunity as the crowd hollered and whooped. And then I listened to Peter describe how Micah paved a way home. Play after play he ran yard after yard to get that ball back to the other side of the field and to safety. First eight yards, then six yards, then another run for another six yards. Slowly and surely moving his team down the field. Another play, another four yards, and then another three and then another two. It was grueling to watch; the yards were harder and harder to come by, but the first downs kept adding up and their troop of warriors kept holding on to their sliver of a lead. Then Micah morphed from runner to blocker, and Peter told my rapt audience of one how this unlikeliest of teams went on to win the championship game they never should have been in when they held on to that last first down and their victory as they stubbornly ran out the clock.

How when the final whistle blew, Peter lifted Jackson so high up into the air that our firstborn was actually scared. That Peter lifted him up over and over as they both cheered like maniacs for our second-born. I could hear the tears in Peter's voice as I sat on the curb and "watched" my son win his first football championship by sheer unshakable force of will.

There would be trophies and speeches and he would come home to our stunned praise and accept it all with a hint of surprise. This boy who always believes that where his words go, his feet will go also. This boy who credits his team and their belief in each other. This boy with all his bulk and often obtuse refusal to accept the way things are. This boy who knows he's a champion on the inside and then dragged himself across the whole world of a football field to prove it to the rest of us.

And at the beginning and end of every game, those boys chanted the same thing. Those warriors, ready for battle—for victory or defeat—would jump up and down, arms strapped around one another as they belted out the words that became their anchor. Those boys who keep helping their parents to grow up. Those boys who still love the game for the game chanted time after time, "Who's got your back? We've got your back! Who's got your back? We've got your back!" And it moves me as powerfully as old-school hymns, as prayer, as a lifetime marriage commitment—because it points to that age-old idea that we're always better together. Always more as a body. Always safer as a community.

So they run out onto that field and accept their victory. They're not the same boys who started together four months ago. They're family now. A brotherhood of bruises and losses and wins. And they stand head and shoulders above our expectations and we love them. Give me football and church and Jesus—not necessarily in that order—every Saturday morning, starting again this fall.

When Parenting Looks Like a 5K Race

*H*e ran next to me the whole time. And I was ashamed I couldn't run as fast as he could. He's eight, and I'll be forty this August. And I watched him choose. He could have run fast and far up ahead where his friends were, where the best times were, where the winners were.

But his glasses kept swiveling in my direction and he kept up a steady stream of chatter when all I could do was wheeze through my aching lungs and wonder how I'd make it another step, let alone another mile.

For the first time in our nearly nine years together, I was the choice in his hand. I felt all vulnerable at being left behind by this son who watches documentaries about Usain Bolt and dreams only of being fast. And I watched him choose me, to run slowly with me.

His slow mother, shy of running and nervous about being at the back alone. His mother who still told him to go on, run at the front, that she'll be fine here by herself.

And over my own raspy conversation and pumping knees, his answer floated back on the breeze like so much grace: "But I want to run with you, Mom."

And parents ran past us, dragging crying kids, snarling under their breath that they should "keep up already. Stop walking." My son looked over and caught my eye every time I shame-facedly confessed that I needed a break to walk for a while, and he told me, "That's fine, Mom. That's fine. This is called a run-walk 5K race, so walking is totally fine."

And then he'd lean over and hug me and we'd walk together on the side of the trail. There is fast and there is kind and that day my son was both. Just not at the same time.

We ran past an old detention center and both gazed up at the guard tower and broken spotlights, the windowpanes all shattered by rocks thrown by kids or detainees or who knows who.

We ran single file along stubbled trails of tall grass and over bridges and down rocky hills—me worrying he'd trip and him flying fast down the spitting stones laughing, all blond hair and grace.

We ran and breathed and ran. Blue sky. Green rough grass. A cutting breeze that chilled us when we arrived too early at seven this morning, an hour before race time. We ran and we walked and always he was right there beside me, checking in and pushing me and encouraging me and telling me over and over, "I love you, Mom. I just can't stop saying how much I love you 'cause you run with me."

And I loved him back in my aching chest that felt sure it couldn't do another mile and then it could. Because my eight-year-old believed in me.

He tells me he's small for his age, and I ask him why he thinks so.

"It's what all the kids say," he tells me.

But when we cross the finish line—him cheering me on the whole way, every hard, burning step—all I can think is, *You're a giant, son. You're a giant of a man to me.*

All Hail the Sidelines Moms

*I*t's too early on a Saturday morning and the gym is still cold. There haven't been enough basketball games in here yet to have raised the thermostat to body temperature and I wish I were still home in bed. I have a coffee in hand and very little energy to scrape together much enthusiasm for this game. The team has been losing, and losing gets old after a while. And I'm not allowed to cheer loudly because it embarrasses Micah, so I'm leaning against the back wall of the gym on the top row of the bleachers and I'm already counting down till this will be over.

I'm sitting alone, aside from Zoe (and she has her dolls and another of the little sideline sisters to play with), and I'm thinking that at least I can get some reading done. But then slowly the air changes. Because there's a mom on the very front row of the bleachers and she's decided that my son, my stubborn son who is more awkward on the basketball court than his bulk is on the football field, is going to be her mascot. And so begins the first of many games when she cheers at squad volume for my son. And he lets her. And he *loves* it.

I lift my head up from my screen and I see how his back straightens, how his knees pump with speed every time he runs by her on the court, and I slowly lower my phone in amazement. "Yes, that's my big boy, Micah!" she yells at him, and he leaps forward for the ball and suddenly his heels are on fire and his lethargy a thing of five minutes ago and this is a brand-new player. I feel my cheeks start to tug into a smile as I look down the stands at the woman who is cheering for my son. I will learn later that she's from Nigeria by way of France and she lives up to every syllable of her name, which she tells me with a big grin is Comfort. She is irresistible, and my son and I both warm to her welcome.

And the season's dynamics change as she gathers a group of sideline moms to her, game after game, and we become united in our loud voices and unembarrassed cheers for our kids as they lose game after game. We believe, regardless of what the scoreboard says, that there is magic happening down there on the court. And there is. There is a team of boys who are backed by an immovable group of mothers who, led by Comfort, put into words all the things young men need to believe about themselves.

"You got this!"

"Yes! You can do it!"

"Don't quit. Stick to it   you got this!"

"It's not time to give up yet!"

"Yes! I saw what you did!"

"We see you!"

Saturdays become like a church for sports, the place where I go to remember the power of speaking truth and grit into our kids. The reminder that mother love is a fierce beast. And I sit every Friday night and Saturday morning in this huddle of unshakable belief that our small humans are becoming exactly who they need to be and that this basketball game is part of that journey.

This is one of the most meaningful things that sports has given my kids: other moms. Other loud, proud voices in their heads. Other words of encouragement. Other screams and whoops of excitement. These are the moms who yell for their kids and every other kid on our (mostly losing) basketball team every weekend. They know each boy by name. They know his strengths. They recognize his accomplishments. They get on their feet, yelling courage across the court. We are a posse of voices saying all the things that every heart longs to hear echo through his being—this belief that great things are possible in the face of great losses.

And it's not only on the side of basketball courts. There are moms who have cheered for years across baseball fields and soccer pitches and at the edge of football fields. These are women who have flung light and life into the dark fear of losing or getting hurt, high into the air like a thousand fireworks to come crashing down in love and expectation over the heads of our kids. They know each child's unique quirks and recognize when to cheer and when to give a kid space to deal with his disappointment. They have been the best part of a thousand Saturdays of sports. If my kids were to lose every single game this season but walk off the court with these women's voices in their heads, I'd call that a big win.

How they champion and call out what they see inside those boys is what counts, more than what the scoreboard says. How they model respect inside their enthusiasm, how they accept the call after a sometimes bad call by the refs, how they applaud with just as much thrill for the opposing team who finally scores a goal, how they pack snacks and coloring pencils for the little siblings, and how they remember each child's name is a testimony to the impact a mother can have on the children of otherwise strangers.

We have sat side by side in the heat and the pouring rain and the doubt of experienced sideline eyes, wondering if a win is still possible to pull off against long odds. We've become each other's faith on the days when we're sure we'll lose again, and we've taken comfort in each other anytime one of our kids has been the one to make the mistake that costs the team a win. We know how it feels, and we're experienced at lending each other the words of encouragement we know we'll need to pass along to our own kids again sometime in the future.

We have had the sacred honor of bearing witness to how our kids also encourage and comfort each other, how they lean on each other on the bad days in the worst games. The nights when my younger son has stood with his head pressed against the back of the dugout, all hope slumped out of his shoulders. And before the moms could say anything, his big brother and teammate has come to stand with arm around him. No words spoken between the two. Just that arm draped across a brother's shoulder, that comfort of presence that says all the things that need saying without using words. And we moms, we've been the ones in our folding chairs passing unspoken looks between one another as we bear witness to this act of love. This more-beautiful-than-words camaraderie that is the heartbeat of teamwork.

This is what we do. We split the disappointment and the joy and the popcorn and the water bottles and the praise. Then we pack it all up again until next week, when we'll all be back at the sidelines to do the church of believing in our kids, against all odds, again.

I Can't Believe What I Saw
You Do Last Night

I watched you win gold last night. I didn't think you would. I'm going to cry as I remember this. But I'm going to write it down, because some photographs are better captured in words. The kind I need to help me properly see how you looked when you crossed that finish line.

I didn't know what to tell you last week when you promised me you were going to grow up to win an Olympic gold. I didn't know how to encourage you while also telling you the truth. Because you're nearly eleven, and you and I spend more time talking about the real things of life and love and the dreams of the man you're going to grow into than we could when you were only six.

We talk in the car and I work hard to be honest. To tell you the truth. Because the truth is a safe place and it's a strong place and it's the place I want you to build your home, my son.

You were born under the Southern Cross. The purple jacarandas celebrated with waving arms and a royal carpet the day we drove you up the driveway and home. Church family and faraway family poured into my father's house for weeks and months after your birth. We were living in the small cottage behind my parents' house, and it became a sanctuary. Even if it was a sleep-deprived one.

We were besotted with you from the beginning. You took your first steps under those jacarandas. We moved back to the States but always kept returning to South Africa in the long dark Michigan winters to be met with South African summer, tea and scones, jasmine and jacaranda trees.

Two years ago I raced you on my old high school track underneath the bright lights. You'd heard all the stories about your mom, the track star in her own mind, who ran the hundred meter, two hundred meter, eight hundred meter, and the four-by-four relay. You'd heard the stories and you wanted to get your own feet onto that track to see if you had it in you.

Everyone was there: two carloads of family as you and I took our spots at the two-hundred-meter starting line under the bright lights. Just that ring of family cheering a private, crazy moment between a mom and her eight-year-old son as we hurled ourselves around the track.

I'd thought I'd go easy on you. I didn't want you to be embarrassed in front of your ouma and oupa and cousins. But instead you set your face like flint and you flew. You flew, my son. And it occurred to me too late that I had miscalculated and needed to pick up my pace to catch you. To catch up to the boy of my blood and my bones and my DNA with a love for speed.

But my knees groaned and the stitch in my side told me I was out of shape and then out of time, and you blazed across the finish line, and Karabo and Lulu and Mo and Micah and Zoe and all the family were whooping and hollering as I laughed myself into a shocked second place.

Do you remember that night? I'll never forget it. How the sky was black and a few stray stars made it through the halo of bright track lights and we ran on the grass that was too long because it wasn't track season yet. But we ran anyway.

You ran again yesterday.

You ran at your first track meet on a beautiful asphalt track under bright-blue American skies, and I stood across from the starting line, behind the fence, with my heart in my throat. I was crying before the starting gun fired.

Because there we were, decades after my own track meets, and my eighteen-year-old self never would have believed it. But there we both were, the me I'd been in high school and the me I am now, both watching my son take his mark at the start of the eight hundred meter.

My race. The race I've run ragged and won and lost and won, with my dad never missing a single meet. He used to come straight from work in tie and suit, and I'd cough and choke at the finish line through his cloud of cologne as he wrapped me into his arms and his proud congratulations and I tried desperately to catch my breath from the ache of the win.

That race will hurt you. I've told you that many times, Jackson.

That race will hurt, and you'll have to race yourself more than you race anyone else. Because you'll have to push yourself to keep going when you want to quit. That's what gold medals are made of.

So you lined up at the start and they fired the gun and my heart leaped forward with the little guy in the glasses as his legs pumped into action.

Track meets hold my heart. Track meets with their wide strip of turf and their wide strip of sky and a hundred parents lined up against the fence yelling for their babies.

"Go, baby, go!" moms scream, and they don't have to use their babies' first names because the kids recognize their moms' voices and they run. They run as hard and as fast and as long as they can and sometimes that still leaves them in dead-last place.

But that doesn't matter to moms, because moms keep shouting; they keep cheering and whooping and hollering long after everyone else has crossed the finish line, because their baby is still running. And the rest of the crowd, they catch the vision and they're swept away with a mother and a single runner and all end up on their feet cheering them both home.

So when that shot shoots you out of the starting blocks, I'm already crying because there's my South African baby running his guts out on an American track under a sapphire sky.

I can tell the pace is fast, and unless you can hang with the first two runners who have broken away from the pack, you won't make it. You'll miss the window. I'm trying to yell, but my throat is so clogged with tears, I can't seem to get the words to make any sound.

But your brother is next to me. And he's hanging over the fence and he's yelling, "Go, Jackson, go. Run! Don't give up!" And then you're coming up the hundred-meter side of the track, heading into the second lap, and you're still there, still hanging on to the top two, and I know that this is when your lungs will start to burn and your legs will tell you they can't keep up.

This is when you win your gold medal, son. At this moment. Not at the finish line. You earn it out there on the far side of the track without any encouragement in your ears, when you keep running even though your lungs and your legs are telling you that they can't.

But you run on.

You run down to the far corner and now all that's left is two hundred meters. And the one remaining boy ahead of you, he makes a break for it. He goes for it. And his arms and legs are flashing and I have a moment where I wonder if you'll decide to stick with him. Because I know it's gonna hurt.

But you do.

You stick like South African–made superglue, and your face turns fierce. Your eyes are huge behind your glasses and I can see your elbows pumping, pumping wildly as you race that boy down the last hundred meters.

And now I'm hanging over the fence. I'm in a long line of parents, and I'm yelling so loud, I can't even remember what I said. I just know I'm crying and I'm yelling and the parents around me stop watching the race and start watching my face and they realize who we're yelling for and they all take up the yell with us.

And you're doing it. Your face hurts and I can see your eyes desperately squinting at that finish line, and your legs are flying. You're flying down the track, son. And now you're passing the last runner and you don't slow down for a second. You don't give an inch. You're earning every second of that finish as you push for home and then there it is.

You pass the finish line first.

And the moms around me are all asking, "Is that your son?" while Micah is yelling, "That's my brother!" And I'm nodding because it's hard to talk, but some words have to be said out loud. They just have to.

"Yes," I say. "That's my son. That's my son, Jackson."

And it is.

My boy who ran with me and now outruns me, and it's my honor. It's the proudest honor of my life to see him run much farther and much faster than I ever did.

Part 7

Why the Middle of Your Friendships Matters

A Pocketful of Friends

S o here's the thing—stuffing myself with new likes and followers, fans and page views, eating up all those hearts and direct messages, tweets and video views, has only ever given me a gut ache. It's never once left me feeling 100 percent satisfied. What it has taught me is that more isn't more when it comes to feeling seen. Deeper not wider is what counts regarding the kind of friends who know what you look like in your unfiltered life.

Here on the other side of forty, I've sunk my roots deep down into the lives of a few women, and for years we've grown together. Grown through our failures and disappointments and dumb mistakes. We've grown closer, not because of doing life together by peering through the tiny one-inch-by-one-inch windows of what is shared online, but because we've opened our back doors and let each other wander in through the stacks of old shoes and muddy boots, kicked off our expectations, and put bare feet up on the furniture. Little by little, we've gone beyond surface conversations into the hallowed halls of those awkward moments, those misunderstandings and hard questions that invite a friendship to the next level. I have a pocketful of those people and they're the treasure that reminds me that we're not required to be impressive; we're invited to be real.

I wear this reminder right above my heart, like a pendant dangling from my favorite necklace—this truth that real is the best part of myself that I can offer anyone else. I wear it when I board planes and go to speak to rooms full of women who might have read my books and maybe gotten the mis-idea that I'm important. I wear this reminder so I won't forget that the most important person in the world is the one I'm talking to right now.

———

I arrived in Sioux Falls, South Dakota, in boots and a coat not nearly warm enough for late October. I had my snacks, my Bible, and the talk I was going to give later that evening. But waiting for me outside baggage claim was Jennifer, a farmer's wife and old friend who understands what homesickness on the road feels like and who tucked me into the comfort of her car, her country roads, corn casserole, fried chicken, and farm life under the wide-open skies of Iowa for the afternoon. Friendship is what anchors you to the realest version of yourself when the rest of the world feels like a bobbing sea of other people's opinions.

———

It's impossible to feel like a caricature when you see yourself reflected in the eyes of a woman who knows what you look like when you're trying not to barf. For me, that place was on an airplane between Washington, DC, and Johannesburg. Joy raised her eyebrows when I stumbled back to my seat next to her, ashen and shaky, and asked me, "Did you just throw up?" And I turned my green face toward her and whispered, "Three times," and I knew we'd never waste time on small talk again.

Katherine drove from Fresno to Visalia in California to come and hear me speak one afternoon. She's known me since the first law-school mixer back in my other life when I was going to be an attorney and accidentally sat on her purse. Funny how a moment like that can become a key plot point in your story. Because she became a central part of mine. Through shared apartments, shared stories about boys, dollar theater movies, my engagement, my wedding, and the afternoon she arrived in Chicago and guessed I was pregnant. Some people know us so well, words are hardly necessary; all those years of doing life together speak for themselves. So as I stepped off the stage at the end of a long and beautiful day spent pouring out every tiny bit of me that I could think of to share with the dear women seated in that gorgeous room, I saw Katherine walking toward me. And suddenly I didn't need to be smart or funny or impressive anymore; I could just be me as I walked into her arms and came home in the middle of a town I still couldn't seem to pronounce properly.

Lisa flew with me to Nashville. Then we rented a car and found our way to the Mexican restaurant the car-rental lady had recommended. It had been a couple of years since I moved away from Lisa's neighborhood and we'd stood on the curb next to our U-Haul, crying and hugging. But we picked right back up where we left off with what's going on with our kids and her decision to quit her executive job to become a teacher and my dream to write books for a living. Over salsa and laughter, we said all the things that fill us up like only good food and good friendship can do and then drove to the wrong hotel and found our way to the right church and she figured out how to set up the signs and book table while I tried not to sweat through my cute denim jacket I was determined not to take off.

It's a sometimes unsettling thing to tell your stories to strangers while one of your best friends is sitting in the front row. She is a barometer for truth, and her presence is the reminder to keep being the truest version of yourself, whether you're sitting in church or on the bedroom floor catching up about that wound you still aren't quite sure you understand how to heal. But when you're together it's always a gift, and sometimes you spend it exploring Broadway in downtown Nashville and admiring all the cowboy boots you can't afford and that really you don't think you're cool enough to wear anyway. But you're together and you're known and those are the things that define you.

—

When the next trip takes me only one state and a couple of hours away, I take my daughter with me. She is growing into one of my dearest friends. She's only seven but she has the high velocity word count of a full-grown woman and I have to be deliberate about crafting time for focusing on all the things she wants to tell me. So we pack our suitcases and head out on our girls' weekend. We stop at the gas station to refuel on petrol and candy, just like my dad used to do with me, and she's surrounded by blankets and stuffed animals in the back seat.

The Friday-afternoon traffic gridlock grinds our trip to a halt, but she keeps right on talking until her curious mind can't compete with the late-afternoon sun and the strong pull to nap. So she curls up and I complete the trip, and when we arrive at the hotel, she pulls her own rolling suitcase toward the building, grinning, and tells me, "Now I feel like a real grown-up lady!" And we two ladies check in and dance around our hotel room and take turns soaking in the tub and climb into our king-size bed to lie back to back in a cocoon of safety and still not silence because she's still talking. Until I tell her I can't keep my eyes or ears open anymore and need to roll over into sleep. For a few heartbeats, she lets me until I feel her arms crawl up and around my body as she snuggles in real close. I can feel the rise and fall of her breathing and then I feel the whisper of her breath in my ear: "That was the best snuggle. I really needed that!" And she turns over and burrows into the blankets as my heart swells and fills all the space between us.

Alice and Judy meet us at the church venue where I'm speaking in the morning. My pastor's wife and her best friend have been on the road since 5 a.m. to come and pray over us and bear witness to my ministry work they've been championing the past year. All those afternoons spent sowing faith and joy and belief into me bubble over in a back room where I watch these three—my two mentors and my girl child—laugh at each other in the mirror as they take turns putting on lipstick and blush. This is love, this generosity that delights in someone else's reflection.

I watch my daughter watching what it looks like to show up for the women in your life. How it looks like laughter and delight and the ability to share in the joy of what God is doing in the life of another woman. There's a rich inheritance waiting for us to claim if only we could get over ourselves and get fully on board with the delight of championing what God is doing in the lives of our sisters. If we can get over our tendency to compare first and encourage second, we'd be so much richer.

Alice and Judy encourage first and second and third and fourth (and you get the point). Until it's late afternoon and I've watched them all day out there in the front row next to my daughter practicing the ministry of amen. They've nodded and agreed and amened throughout each one of my three talks. And when I'm in a long line of greeting and hugging and signing, they stop by with faces on fire with pride and hug me goodbye, and I'm more because of them. I'm fuller because of them. And I'm walking in their footsteps so I can be that for the women who are growing up alongside me. May I offer them the same delighted celebration. May I speak the same words of affirmation. May I be the first in line to tell them, "Well done, little sister."

―――

My mother-in-law flies from Florida and I fly from Baltimore and we meet in Saint Louis, Missouri. Then we rent a car and drive three hours to Poplar Bluff, Missouri. She gives me the gift of her presence at the end of a long travel season. It's a shelter and it's like coming home, even though I'm driving through the rolling landscape of a state I've never visited before.

We stop at the sign that promises home cooking but leave again when we see the tired-looking food and well-used sneeze guards. But one block over they're serving all-day breakfast, and we park ourselves in the booth and order bacon and eggs and hash browns and laugh our way through old stories and new stories, and both our hair is crazy from the wind that comes whipping across the plains today.

Really, I don't call her my mother-in-law, because she's been my mom for years. For decades, actually. She's my mom who's prayed and fasted with me for stubborn kids, for books I'm struggling to write, and for my marriage to her son.

She never comes packing judgy lists when she comes to visit. Instead, she asks me to make her lists of what I most need help with in the house. Yeah, she's that great.

We talked nonstop on our three-hour car ride and she helped me clip my mic pack down my shirt and to the back of my jeans. And she prayed over me like only a mom can before I walked out of the choir room and onto the stage. And when I walked off again, her words were the only ones I wanted to hear. Because who will we believe when they tell us, "Well done"? We will believe our mothers because they've been there for the failures. So we trust them to recognize the nights we stand with both feet planted firmly in our callings, as they're the ones who've prayed us there.

I stood bent over in her arms so I could reach down to her height and let her approval just soak into me. Then we walked down to the fellowship hall for cake and the chance to look women in the eyes and remind them that not only does God love them but He really likes them.

At midnight, after hours of conversation with strangers who now feel like friends, we go to Steak 'n Shake because it's the only place still open, and I crumple into the seat across from her because I'm completely empty and there's nothing left to hold me up anymore. She orders burgers and fries and tells me again how proud she is of me, and all I have to do is receive it and eat it and believe it. I'm so full and so tired and she insists on picking up the check. Because that's what moms do, she tells me. But the table of ladies across the room from us who were also in the pews earlier have already paid for both of us.

So we stumble out into the rain and back to the hotel and it's pouring now and I hug her at my hotel room. I'm just a little girl with a mom who loves her, and it's the biggest feeling of being enough that there is. When we're at the airport the next day, I'm in line to board my flight back to Baltimore and she's down at the other end of the terminal headed to Fort Myers, when I feel a tap on my shoulder. And there she is again, back for one last hug. And I fly home on the wings of family friendship, the dearest kind. You can trust it like you trust your right hand or your beating heart or your breathing lungs. Maybe even more than that.

Because these days I've found my sprained back incredibly untrustworthy. But friends and family? They will hold you up when you can't hold yourself up anymore. And sometimes when all you want to do is lie down, they will be there lying right beside you.

———

After a speaking event in Nashville one October and a short minivan ride back to the hotel, four friends and I rode up the elevator and into a hotel room. I was so tired. I needed out of my skinny jeans and into something comfortable—something that felt like home. I needed heels off and sneakers on. I needed Chapstick and a hairbrush and mostly I needed to close my eyes and find a way to process everything from the day.

Sometimes friendship is a deep conversation. Sometimes it's a shared ugly cry. But sometimes friendship is the gift of not being afraid of silence. With only fifteen minutes before we needed to regroup, we collectively lay down on the beds and tucked ourselves between soft comforters and a soothing layer of safe silence.

As I lay with my back pressed up against the rise and fall of a friend's breathing, I could feel with each inhale and exhale the God who breathed life into us lay Himself down between us. How when we are safe we don't need to fill the spaces with small talk. How we can simply give and receive the gift of shared presence. Our bodies tucked into beds for brief moments of finding rest between our friends and the pillows.

It was the moment from the weekend that sits like a cup of hot chocolate right there, warming the spot beneath my rib cage. This ability to let your guard down in a roomful of women. To warm yourself in their silence. To believe you are known without saying a word. It is a very rare thing. A precious thing that, if you think about it too much or too long, might dissolve right when you try to put your finger on it.

In a decade of serving women, I've heard too many stories of hurts that run deep to ever take safe friendship for granted. I know it now for the treasure it is.

So I lay back to back with Holley. With Kristen in the next bed over and Jacque sitting on the floor and Kaitlyn beside us on a chair, and in each breath, each rise and each fall of our bodies, I could hear the heartbeat of a long friendship. A friendship that lives comfortably now in the silent spaces because it has walked through all the spaces in between. The hard and the sad and the heartbreaking. But always, always with the determined commitment to love, to love, to love.

These word sisters of mine.

I am more because of them. More of a writer. More of a Jesus follower. More of a listener. More of a believer. More of a fighter.

And I am less because of them. Less afraid. Less worried. Less trapped in the cycles of comparison.

So I breathe in and out and watch the late-afternoon sunshine spilling through the soft white cotton curtains, and in two minutes we will all go downstairs for what comes next. But I know, I know with each breath that these sisters will always have my back. And I will always have theirs. And I smile at the small crack in the ceiling tiles, and I put this gift into my pocket.

Instead of the slights and criticisms that I've been so quick to collect over the years, like pebbles filling up my pockets and sometimes spilling out of my mouth. No, today I put this moment, this gift of the safety of silence, the comfort of friendship, into my pocket like a seashell so that later I can take it out again and hold it up to my ear, where I can still hear the echo of what it sounds like to breathe in companionship with my friends. The breath of the beloved, the secure, the seen.

I hold it up to my ear so I can remember what it sounds like. So I can know what it sounds like when it comes time to pass it on.

The Gift of Years and Words

*F*or nearly two decades, ten of us have stayed in touch since we graduated law school. It's unusual. But it's because a few of those women love like superglue. They've kept us all stuck together across time zones and countries and weddings and new babies and new jobs and despair and breakups and chick flicks. Hundreds of chick flicks.

We all graduated from the Notre Dame Law School in the spring of 2001, and somehow we've always held each other's hands since then. Since South Bend I've lived in Chicago, Illinois; Kyiv, Ukraine; Pretoria, South Africa; Owosso, Michigan; Springfield, Virginia; and Hanover, Maryland, and those friends have visited me in every single zip code except one, which was the year I didn't think it would be worth them spending all that money to come see me. Turns out I was wrong.

I joke that they're like the friendship mafia—no one ever gets out. I know. I've tried. There were years I disappeared into my own life and stopped working at keeping in touch. I should have known better, because they simply held on tighter to me. And they didn't let me turtle for too long. They knew better. They knew that friendship is the life preserver you don't realize you need until you need it. And then they were there. Always there.

They've pursued each other through worse than that. They've never given up, never quit, never washed their hands of one another. They are the DNA of what it looks like to keep showing up long after the hope of showing up has left the building.

So when they planned a long weekend away at a rental house on Lake Michigan to celebrate seventeen years of friendship, Peter told me, "You have to go." The calendar told me that we would have just flown in three days earlier from South Africa and my jet lag and motion sickness wouldn't be so sure about getting back on a plane again. But my husband insisted. Everyone was coming in from all four corners of the world and he told me, "You'll regret it. You'll always regret it if you miss this one."

He was so right.

I cashed in all my air miles and bought a ticket and rented a car and drove the familiar stretch of skyway between Chicago and South Bend until I wound my way down the edge of the lake onto a tiny patch of parking area behind an old beach house. There was just one other car already sitting there even though I was the last to arrive. No one was home. I knocked hesitantly and made my way inside. The bathrooms spoke of girls and curls and more makeup than a Sephora store, and the kitchen laughed with empty wine glasses and the stifling hot Michigan sun that covered everything with a layer of humidity.

I shifted from foot to foot. Changed into a cooler T-shirt. Wondered when last I'd seen everyone. One or two at a time over the years, but decades since we were all in one place at one time. I was nervous. Coming home is a strange thing. Coming home to friends who know you but who haven't walked alongside your day-to-day and still own all these memories of the you who you were is so vulnerable. I hovered in the downstairs living room, where it was marginally cooler. And then I heard the front door slam.

I walked down the hall and wondered who'd be there first. I heard the voices, and familiarity pulled a grin around my face and then there they were: the women who have insisted on being my friends for almost two decades now. Who can claim such a thing? This is wealth you can't put into words. I stood in the doorway smiling and put my arms out to Melissa and Shonda, when Katherine came barreling in front of them yelling, "Me first! Me first!" She swept me up in her friendship and welcome and a huge hug and I was home. I shared an apartment with Katherine before I ever shared one with Peter and she has always believed in me, especially when I hadn't believed in myself. We danced at my wedding like only girlfriends can to our favorite chick-flick soundtrack. She is fierce and fiercely loyal and kind, and she was the first friend I made at law school.

Shonda made the first quilt for my first baby and for every baby since. And she's leaned in and cheered for each of my book babies and insisted that we could both write fiction if we put our minds and our time to it. Amiee was the person I called when I went into labor with Zoe, and she came to watch the boys while I went to meet my daughter. Maureen looked me dead in the eyes when I couldn't decide if I should stay at the law firm job I hated or go with my new husband on his adventure to Ukraine and told me, "If you don't go with Pete, I'll never be able to respect you again." She changed the course of my career and my marriage, all for the incredibly better.

Their eyes brim with these memories, and their arms hug me with all the new ones we're going to make this weekend. And how is it possible that Jill has seven kids and still wears the same tiny body she had in law school? Marjie is like what champagne would look like if it took human form, and her joy bubbles over into each of us as she does her late-night body rolls. Melissa is laughing so hard, she can't breathe as she watches Marjie. And later she will remind us of the rules of poker in her southern drawl. Becky's brain is brilliant and fascinating and she can run marathons as well as advise you on patent law. She always has time for you, and her faith in her friends is a thing you can hold in your hand and put in your pocket.

Janelle will get us out the door and to a restaurant on time and give us all the best menu choices to pick from for each meal. She is driven and so sharp and she'll be the perfect person to share a bed with, never snoring, as we both fall exhausted into sleep after night after night of speed dating our friends to catch up on years of missed stories. Maureen listens with her whole body to what you say. You feel as though even her fingers are quieting themselves so her eyes can hold you in their warm welcome, where she is always a safe place to share your failures or your victories. She wants to hear both from you. And then she wants to convince you to run a marathon with her or eat more Greek yogurt.

Amiee will laugh so hard at your stories and share so many of her own, you'll half believe she is some red-lipped super-secret spy who has stepped into your real life. All her years with the State Department mean she can casually say things like, "Oh, that weekend doesn't work for me. I'll be in Pakistan," while in the same breath telling you all about how much she loves being able to order Starbucks from her iPhone app. And because she's based in DC for a couple years, she'll come and spend weekends with us and never get tired of listening to my dreams and then actually believing them. We'll share Hallmark movies and SkinnyPop popcorn and good wine and teach Zoe the joy of the cheesy rom-com.

Good night, the glory of these women takes my breath away! I'm amazed how they walk in courage and aren't afraid to tell it like it is, yet you'll never ever doubt how much they love you. We decide to take some group photos at sunset. (Or maybe I boss them into the idea. Who's to say?) But Becky brings her camera and we set and reset and test lighting and send ourselves leaping into the sky as the auto timer sends the flash winking at us. There is this wild patch of beauty there on the shores of Lake Michigan and only our cameras bear witness to it. Except that of course we all see and will all remember, because Shonda will make us each a photo book.

We will remember how Katherine leaped into the most epic photobomb of all time. We will remember how we laughed and the sunset spilled across our faces and into our new memories and how we hardly cared about being late for dinner but definitely cared about not making Janelle late.

There are women who will tell you that there's just no point in trying to have girlfriends. That competition or comparison or distance will kill off the friendship. To them I say, "Yes, that is a very real risk, but try anyway."

Because one day your mother might die or you might discover a tumor or that your kid has started lying at school and you will need your friends like you need air to gasp into your shocked lungs. You will need them to remind you who you are underneath all this weight of disappointment you're carrying. You'll need them to come over with girlie wine and cheese and crackers and sit beside you on the sofa as you dream your unrealistic dreams with them, and you'll need to hear them say that they believe in you.

Their belief will be like a dream catcher that wards off your fears and gives you their own faith to put into your pocket. One you take out and believe in on the days it gets dark and hard to see the future. That's the kind of friendship that can't be taken for granted, because it is its own organism. It doesn't need you; it now exists above and beyond you. It has grown into a living, breathing, believing being, and you can hold its hand on the days your nightmares or your daydreams come true. It won't let go. This is the stuff of faith, this kind of friendship.

On our last day at the beach, Katherine says we need to mark this weekend with something tangible, something meaningful. I'm surprised, because she might be the least sentimental of all of us, but when I'm at my pilgrimage to Meijer grocery store, I pick up note cards and envelopes like she asked me to do. Then we wind our way through backstreets and side streets, past tourists, and back to the house. She explains how we're each going to be assigned a particular set of colored note cards and envelopes and how there's one card for each person represented. And we're to write down what we love about each other. And on our last night together, we'll go around our circle and give each other the gift of words. We'll put into words and down on paper all the ways we see the wonder in the life of each woman.

So we spend our last hours together spread out across the deck and the living room and the kitchen, with Melissa's speaker blaring our favorite nineties tunes as we try to capture the magic of each woman on the tiny surface of a four-by-six-inch note card. It's impossible and it's essential. Some girls have taken their cards down to the beach. Katherine and I fret that they may not get done in time, but of course when Katherine gives you an assignment, you complete it. They come trooping back, sweating sunscreen and ink, and it's hard to condense ten friends into less than a thousand words each. But we do. Slowly. One by one we write down the ways we love one another.

There are snacks—popcorn and cherries and assorted nuts, cheeses, and drinks—and we write. Sometimes someone bursts out laughing, and we use those silly celebrity magazines (that we all still love) like lap desks to support our writing. This is us, all in one room set to the serenade of delight in one another.

Of course, it's awkward to have a roomful of women all speak out loud what they love about you, what they see in you, what they appreciate about you. But it's necessary. And it's sacred. And it's impossible to do with dry eyes. So when all the note cards are ready, we just launch right into telling the beautiful truth about each woman as we see her. And of course we sob our way through it all, strengthened by good wine and the friend next to us leaning over to rub our back, pass a tissue, or laugh at the unexpected wonder of being affirmed.

I have to leave first because I have an early afternoon flight, so they open the faucet and just pour down affirmation all over me until I'm streaming love and tears and the deep delight of being known and seen by the people who've known me the longest. I pack all their note cards into my carry-on, making it the most important piece of luggage I bring home with me.

It's still the first thing I pack. For any trip, anywhere. That ragged little envelope filled with the words of ten of my best friends in the rainbow collection of cards. Those words are my shield against what anyone else might say. They are my bodyguards, protecting me against the unkind words of people who might not know me. They are the only reviews that matter to me, because they are written first in love before anything else. They are my greatest friendship treasure and they walk up onto any stage with me to remind me that the same girl who stands in front of that room was loved and accepted a long time ago and doesn't need to earn the approval of anyone else anymore.

I hope you have those friends too. I hope you hold on to their words with both hands. I hope you've spent years refusing to let them quit your circle. I hope your circle has stretched. I hope that even after friendship has hurt you, you haven't quit it altogether. I hope you've held on to the belief that strangers are just friends waiting to discover what they have in common. Here's to the awkward business of saying hello and showing up for book club or running club or in the break room at work or the nursery at church. I believe investing in friendship will dramatically raise your joy levels and also give you fresh insights into how to pair tall boots and skinny jeans as well as teach you everything you need to know about the Instant Pot and raising teens. The surprise of friendship is how it will recommend new fall TV shows while also making you see yourself for who you really are and still always championing who you are growing up to be. Write the note cards. Say the words out loud. Tell your friends why you love them. And let yourself be seen. It's been one of the most satisfying parts of my middle. Discovering that I am not here alone.

Church in the Parking Lot

Sometimes public speaking comes easy, and sometimes you straight-up think you're going to throw up from nerves beforehand. A couple of months ago I was invited to speak at an event that had me sandwiched in between two of my most beloved, most admired mentors. From my perspective it was like a panic sandwich with a side of fear, nausea, and trembling. It was truly awful.

I'm not overexaggerating, because usually I absolutely love the chance to share my story with other women. But for the weeks and then the days and then the hours leading up to this particular event, I built up the kind of cold sweat of dread that could have fueled several full-length horror flicks. You know what I'm talking about here, yes? You've faced your own Everest at work or in public speaking or during that project you're trying to launch or that deadline you're trying to hit or that opportunity you're so afraid you're going to blow? And you keep running back and forth to the bathroom, and sleep is impossible, and there's a hamster wheel running in your head showing all the ways this could go wrong. Yes, you know what I'm saying, it was *exactly* like that.

No matter how much I prepared or how much I studied, I couldn't stop my hands from shaking or my brain from telling me that this was a big, *big*, BIG almighty mistake and I needed to find a way out. I mean, messing up is one thing. Messing up in front of women you've admired for years is something else entirely. I'd already had a small taste of it earlier in the year, and I was not keen on taking another bite out of that particular humble pie.

So during the team dinner beforehand, I picked at my food and couldn't muster up the stomach for the bountiful buffet of my favorite of all cuisines: Mexican. That's the panic level I was at. I was legitimately worried that all the chips and salsa would surface again at an extremely awkward moment if I indulged in them, so I sat at my table and drank water instead. I made quiet small talk with the people next to me, who likely thought I was incredibly shy or incredibly stuck up since I couldn't seem to function like a normal human or make normal conversation. So then I just pretended to read the event program over and over, all the while wondering what kind of foolishness had led the event organizers to trust me with their stage.

I was scheduled to give the 7:00 p.m. keynote. By 5:30 p.m. I'd started to hyperventilate. My boss and friend, Janie, had picked me up from the hotel, where I'd gone to try to decompress and gain some small rational part of my brain back. But instead all that happened is I sat in the car next to her, repeating over and over again, "I don't know if I can do this. I just don't know if I can do this." Janie seemed to believe that I could, and she let me blast a South African version of "Amazing Grace" in her car as she drove me toward my fate.

My one small comfort was the understanding that the teacher I secretly wished I could grow up to be and who would be speaking on the same stage at the next morning's keynote was away at a dinner in her honor that night. So I was holding on to the slim hope that at least I would be spared making a fool of myself in front of her. I was wearing a mic pack and false eyelashes, because when in the South, baby, if one can't pull off big hair, the least one can do is get lash extensions. Hovering in the tiny room backstage I tried not to appear as weird as I felt on the inside. There were three kind gals waiting to share their testimonies ahead of my talk and I know I should have done much more than offer them the dead-eyed smile that I dredged up from the black cave where my soul had gone to hide.

I had to keep getting up to pee in the tiny bathroom, which I'm sure left nothing to the imagination for everyone else sitting right next to the door. And the tech guys thought it was funny to joke with me about potty sound effects and I'm sure my laugh was weird and hollow. Then just as I was starting to accept my reality, one of the techies came into the room and said in surprise that he hadn't realized that the next morning's speaker and my favorite Bible teacher—she of the big hair and my obsessive love, admiration, and unrelenting hope that she might adopt me and feed me chicken and dumplings in her kitchen one day— had, in fact, just entered the building.

I almost lost my non-dinner on the spot.

I lost all the color in my face.

And one of the techies suddenly got worried and leaned over to ask if I was okay. "No," I croaked. "I am *not okay*."

He backed away and smiled kindly and then totally lied and told me it was going to be fine. Because *he* wasn't the one who had to walk out onto that stage in front of a few thousand people, including the woman I had always wanted to teach like when I grew up. No, he didn't have to go do that. I did.

It was bad. In my sheer terror I started Googling random Hebrew and Greek words on my phone. I had a sudden panic attack that I was going to unintentionally commit heresy onstage in front of her. That she was going to pull me aside afterward and gently, tenderly, in her southern accent, rebuke me in the name of the Lord. I thought that if I could at least quote the meaning of some ancient words in Greek or Hebrew I could fake it. That I could somehow fake myself and the audience into believing that I was qualified to be on that stage.

It was not pretty. And I had to mentally slap myself and get a grip and put my phone down and yank my jeans up again and walk onto that stage and try not to make eye contact with the one teacher I respected more than almost any other in the world. I managed not to trip. That gave me at least a semblance of courage. And I had my big ol' family-sized purple faux-leather-cover Bible in my hands to anchor me. And I started to speak, to tell a story about my firstborn and his passion for sneakers. I was surprised to hear my own voice and took courage by tucking my self-consciousness into the curve of my son's dream for his own shoe store. And before I knew it, I had smiled at the delightful teacher in the bright-pink jacket in the front row and she grinned right back and I didn't die. The wall of love and protection built around me that afternoon held true.

You see, earlier in the day three friends read the terror in my face and pushed back their own agendas and sat themselves down around me. We were in the massive auditorium after hearing from another brave teacher and we were heading out in separate directions. They were going to workshops and I was going back to my room to be near a toilet in case I actually did throw up.

But they caught what was hidden underneath my casual tone and called me out on it. And then they gave me the gift that women carry with them. They gave me the gift of their presence and their precious time. They raised up a wall of protection around me with their prayers and their tight hugs and the circle they sat in around me as they spoke words of courage from our Father God. And I held their hands and held on to their conviction with both my own hands, like a life preserver. As though I could climb into their brave and make it mine from the inside out.

We live in a world where the Enemy wants to trick us women into building walls between one another. Walls of comparison and insecurity and jealousy. But we are mentored by a God who builds walls of protection around His friends. A God who willingly walked into the dark to trade His life for the lives of His friends. Those who betrayed Him, denied Him, and abandoned Him. Those who hadn't been born yet and those who don't even know His name. He laid down His life and in so doing raised a fortress of protection with walls thicker than the castles of our fairy tales—solid and unshakable—around His family of friends, doubters, haters, and naysayers.

Stacey, TeriLynne, and Erin raised their voices and their prayers and thick solid walls of belief around me. They believed in me when I didn't believe in myself. That changed everything. It changed me that night. Because their words and their wall held true. It didn't take away the scared, but it gave me the faith to walk onto that stage anyway from inside a place of safety. A place where my fear couldn't strangle me. A place where my message could take a big gulp of air and take flight. Those three women built me up with bits of themselves and their faith, so when I walked onto the stage, I walked in their shoes, by their faith and not by my own sight. And it felt more than a bit like a miracle.

The next day they took me out for Mexican food for lunch. I told you, miracle friends. On the way back we weren't quite ready to quit the conversation that had started over queso and guac, so we parked in a spot of sunshine outside the convention center and for the next forty-five minutes had ourselves some church inside their rental car.

Generosity is the perfect dessert course. It fills up all the tiny nooks and crannies of emptiness that might still linger after lunch or after a year or two of hard work and always wondering if you're still somehow missing the mark.

But those women, those three and the others from their women's ministry team also in the car with us, parked right on my heart and simply opened up a faucet of generous encouragement and poured it over my life until I was drenched. Until I was soaked through to the skin, to the soul, with affirmation and confirmation that only the women who've known me for years can speak with any kind of conviction.

We live in a culture that struggles to take compliments. We shrug them off like awkward gnats. But that afternoon I dug in with what felt like a shovel to spoon all that love and validation into my belly, and it was so, so good. We don't realize how hungry we are to hear from our sisters the words "Well done." When spoken they are generosity incarnate and they can fill up our empty places and give us the strength to keep walking into spaces that scare us.

And I have been scared. I know how that feels. I have woken up at night sweating and frightened of my own shadow, of my critics, of the voices in my head, and of the doubts in my soul. I have a 4 a.m. hamster wheel of regret that I get up and ride as regularly as I'm sure you do too. I was not prepared to be welcomed and approved of in that way. If it sounds foreign to you, it felt foreign to me too.

So I sat in the front seat with my neck craned around to meet the faces of the women who really saw me. And I loved them. I loved them for their willingness to make this time. To add bricks to the walls of protection and friendship they'd laid around me. To build on the strong foundations of years spent trusting one another, championing one another, and taking turn after turn saying aloud what strengths they saw in each other. It's the nonrepayable gift. It's billionaire-level generosity. It's gold. All you can do is say thank you and pack that moment into your pocket so that you can be sure to pass it on to another sister. This delight in what she does. This commitment to stand in the gap for her. This joy at seeing her succeed.

A thousand compliments from strangers will never carry the weight of one word spoken from a trusted friend. Later that night I would sit in my sweatpants and my Detroit Tigers sweatshirt and call my oldest, dearest online friend, Ann, and cry. Because we've moved far beyond internet connection and into each other's real everyday lives and have lived our highest highs and deepest lows spanning the last decade together. Because sometimes what you've lived in a short, intense burst of time is just too big for words. It's too beautiful to try to define. It's too sacred to speak out loud. So you just cry and mumble and gush and stumble, and there's a friend on the other end who simply listens and that's enough. That's what coming home can feel like, even when you're standing on the carpet of a hotel room miles from where you started.

So I sent her message after message of what that wildly unexpected weekend had looked like and she replied with message after message of delight. The deep belief of an old friend who has always believed that God actually can be trusted with our stories. The friend who has let you step into her faith on the days your own has refused to walk you forward. You can stand in her shoes and remember what it feels like to believe.

Ann has believed for me on too many days to count. She has believed and loved and listened to a thousand scared, angry, wounded phone calls. Over mornings doing our hair or drinking our tea or in person sleeping on each other's sofas, there has been honesty and acceptance and always the guarantee that nothing will ever be treated as anything other than a gift. Each other's pains and joys and secrets—these are the offerings of a friendship that's left permanent marks.

Deep and wide, they're the foundation of an old friendship. The story of being known and knowing another woman by laying down your armor, your tendency to get defensive or spiky or threatened. To refuse to see her success as anything other than your own victory. To hold her hand across the miles or in the parking lot or the row of chairs in the back of a big hall and listen to her fear and then speak back to her all the courage you know that lives inside her.

This is what we do here in the middle years. This is how we make up for all the time and the fights wasted in middle school. This is how we lean in and encourage our sisters to rise up. Right where they are. Right where they're headed. With us always a faithful wall of protection around them on the hardest days, the best days, and all the in-between days too. We cheer and cry till our throats are raw, and in the morning we are closer than we were the day before. It's a holy thing. This choosing to love our friends as much as we love ourselves. This refusing to be intimidated by them. This doing church together, wherever we are.

In minivans or kitchens, on couches or in living rooms with carpets dredged in crushed Cheerios. When was the last time you slowed down enough to let a sister know she mattered to you more than your schedule? When was the last time you let someone love you by offering her your broken heart and trusting her to superglue it back together, piece by piece, with words of safety, honesty, encouragement, and belief in you? When last were you vulnerable enough to swing the front door of your life wide open so friends could step right inside your business and put their feet up on the furniture and share the popcorn and the hard stories? Sometimes it might end in misunderstanding, but sometimes, and these are the times that make nonsense of every other bumpy time, sometimes you will find yourself in the company of friends who really do have all your very best dreams at heart. And they will say the words that make you feel seen and believed and they will send you back out into the world, stronger, braver, and more determined to keep walking, one foot at a time, deep into the purposes you feel the most strongly called toward. And you will know you're not walking alone. You never were.

Part 8

Why the Middle of Your Faith Matters

For the Thomases

I've struggled with doubt here in the middle years more than at any other time in my life. More than when my mom died the week after I turned eighteen. More than when my dad remarried a stranger I'd never met while I was living overseas. More than when my dad got divorced and before he met the woman who would put our family back together and I went back to living overseas. More than during my worst jobs and the hardest stretches of my own marriage.

Here in the middle place, where life feels as if it's slowly rocked toward some kind of equilibrium, where I feel happy—and more than that, where I feel content—there are days I also feel strangely and inexplicably riddled with doubt in a way I never was when it would have made a lot more sense.

But I also feel riddled with faith. While I may have questioned many things about what I believe, I've never questioned Jesus Himself. Faith and doubt seem to have become dance partners here in my middle years, twisting themselves around and around in a double helix of belief and questions that quickstep through my spiritual DNA and my daily routine. As I'm driving the car pool or talking to a friend who's catching me up on her painful story that included a trip to the emergency room as well as one to the police station to report a runaway in a single week, my doubt takes the lead. But when I listen to the messages of encouragement, of radical prayer, of meal trains set up to put our Crock-Pots where our mouths are, faith leads out.

This is always where I meet up with Jesus again. Through the stories of other people. The messy, ugly, upside-down, sometimes crazy-funny, crazy-hopeful, crazy-beautiful stories of people who keep showing up for each other. These stories loosen the knots tied around my chest and help me take a deep breath of belief again.

And here in the middle place, I've loved the freedom to keep expanding my library of learning to include more and more fiction writers, poets, artists, moviemakers, musicians, teenagers, and college students. I've loved seeing the world through the eyes of middle school history teachers, executive assistants, nurses, rocket scientists, pastors' wives, film directors, and stay-at-home moms. Leaning in to listen to the stories of faith and doubt from creatives across the globe and the people here in my real-life zip code was like turning my head and discovering that I wasn't the last person in the back row at church. No, I was smushed up in the very middle of the most fascinating collection of crazy stories chock full of sadness and confusion and elation and fear and stupidity and completely ridiculous redemption. Because church has never been four walls and a few hundred rows; it has always been a million people in all their shapes and sizes with all their messy and mostly messed-up stories. The church is a place with skin on. It's not brick and mortar; it's skin and bones.

And church stories, like Bible stories, should always welcome the doubters. This past year I have developed a kinship with so-called doubting Thomas from the Bible, who said he wouldn't believe that Jesus had risen from the dead till he'd seen it with his own eyes, till he'd put his own fingers in those nail marks and that scarred body. It's the church that labeled Thomas a doubter. Jesus simply called him a friend and showed up and let old Thomas have at it. What if we made more room for doubt and less demand for fired-up, frame-worthy faith?

What if we were just allowed to lean in and listen to the stories and discover the redemption tucked under the unexpected corners without actually having it all dissected for us and spelled out in bullet points? What if we got to know Jesus as a person and not just a caricature? His personhood is His most fascinating quality. How the being who claimed to not just be *a* god but *the* God came and walked around in our literal shoes wearing our actual skin and feeling our emotions and living the creation He'd breathed into existence from the inside out. My twelve-year-old gets it when he exclaims with a fist slammed into palm for emphasis, "I mean, Mom! I mean, that's wild! That's so wild that God would come do that."

We're driving down Forest Avenue, and it still strikes me as pretty wild here, too, at the middle of a long life lived neck deep in church. I've been sitting in Sunday school and church and Bible study and small groups and women's groups and around our dining room table learning about Him since as far back as I can remember. And it still never gets old to have a teacher blow my mind with a connection I've never seen before, a translation that ping pongs bright new realizations around my head. I love seeing how this God-man manages to keep creeping under my skin in unexpected ways that make sense of unexpected days here on earth.

But hand in hand with that comes the relearning, here in the middle years, of one of my favorite things about Jesus that I first really grasped when I was a kid: that He really likes people. That we're not talking about a God who keeps His distance. We're introduced to a God who likes to get up close and personal. Who is interested in us. Who really likes these humans He's created in His image. We learn that if He likes us enough to die for us, He must really like our weird little foibles and how some of us snore and what our quirky styles are and how some of us carry our babies on our backs wrapped around with bath towels and some use Ergobaby carriers. That some struggle with math problems and count on their fingers or can make fried chicken so hot that it feels like even your bones are sweating.

Sometimes surrounded by all my Bibles and Bible studies and study books and commentaries and Christian self-help, I forget that I believe in the God who doesn't just love us, rescue us, redeem us . . . but who actually likes us.

He *likes* us.

I was sitting in an Afghan restaurant on a Tuesday afternoon because I was indulging in a bit of my own figurative hair petting and back rubbing after a couple of weeks spent shuttling between the dentist, the endodontist, and the oral surgeon. I had already been through a tooth extraction and was still facing a bone graft and implant as well as a root canal re-root (how is this even a real thing?), so that afternoon I found myself driving up to the best Afghan lunch buffet in Columbia, Maryland. I pulled in and found a table and dished up rice and more rice and samosas and sweet squash and chicken malai and crisp salad with tangy dressing and a Diet Coke. And then I took out my idea of comfort reading to go with my comfort food.

It's the book I'd gone home to after a few weeks of spending time teaching at women's conferences: *The Sacred Diary of Adrian Plass, Christian Speaker, Aged 45 3/4* by Adrian Plass.* And it was his words as well as the naan bread that comforted and filled my soul. His reminder that Jesus genuinely likes us. Even on the days we're disappointed in Him. Even on the days we cry and climb up into His lap like desperate, exhausted toddlers, with tears streaming down our red faces as we pound on His chest for all the ways we believe He's let us down. Still He holds us. He lets us rage until we storm out all our fear and frustration and fall asleep in His arms, and He just holds us. Holds us and rocks us for as long as it takes to let all His love for us seep back into our bones.

With a mouthful of rice and sweet squash, I stared at the pages and felt the tears crowding into my eyes. Like they couldn't wait to spill all my relief onto the table. I think here in the middle, more than at any other time, I'm so desperate to remember what it felt like at the beginning. When I was a little six-year-old girl who literally believed what her parents had taught her: that Jesus was coming back for her. So she went to stand at the window of her house, waiting to spot Jesus coming to find her. A little girl who didn't feel constantly unqualified or deeply exhausted at all the things everyone else seemed to be doing for Jesus that she wasn't. Who could sing with the conviction of the very young that "Jesus loves me, this I know, for the Bible tells me so." It seems these days there are so many ways we're measured, so many ways we measure ourselves, that it becomes hard to measure up. We stop being little children loved by a Father who thinks we're rad and instead start trying to win approval from the other people in our Father's family.

---

* Adrian Plass, *The Sacred Diary of Adrian Plass, Christian Speaker, Aged 45 3/4* (Grand Rapids, MI: Zondervan, 2005), 58.

And we forget that they're not the boss of us and also that they're loved by Him not because of anything special they've done either but simply because He made them.

Here in the grown-up years, we've become experts at keeping score. So we imagine God must be doing the same. And we worry we're disappointing Him, because we measure His aptitude for disappointment by how easy it can be to disappoint the people around us. But maybe He's not looking for a checklist of good behavior from us; maybe He's simply looking for us to throw open the upstairs window and gaze out at the road with the anticipation of a child who can't wait to run into her father's arms. Or the hope of a disciple who keeps looking around every corner, craning his eager neck because he's always expecting to see the God-friend who promised He'd be back soon. Maybe He isn't interested in our tattling on one another as much as He's eager to hear us boasting to Him how much we delight in each other, and how we're in it together—this waiting for His return.

Here in the middle I can't keep trying to out-Christian the people around me. And I don't want to. And I'm not qualified to. I'm tired of trying to look like a version of myself that might make some folks happy even while it will rub other folks wrong. It all makes me exhausted. It's impossible to pretzel ourselves into a one-size-fits-all stamp of approval. Once upon a time it was enough to be just God's daughter who was excited to see Him. I've started to wonder if that's still enough. If that was always enough.

The chicken malai filled my belly, and that memory filled my soul. What if even here in the tired forties there is still a little girl with mousy brown hair who can fling open her window and look out across the driveway lit up by the sky and expect to see a God come running for her? What if He has never stopped? What if He's always been running and I got distracted by all the things I thought I was supposed to be doing for Him and wandered off the path trying to prove that I deserved Him? What if all I have to do is open my arms and look up to find Him there waiting, beaming down, ready to swing me up into His arms and around and around?

My children ask similar questions. The difference is that they're not embarrassed to ask. They don't think the questions somehow disqualify them. They ask because asking means you want to get to know someone. And they want to get to know this God whom Zoe says she's never heard from personally and whose voice she wishes she could hear. It's right here, I tell her. It's right here beating in your chest with each heartbeat that pumps life around your bones. It's here in your very being, my daughter, this voice that sings over you while you're sleeping. This assurance that you are loved by a God who delights in you and calls you good not because of what you've done but because of who you are. Because you are His and He delights in you.

When my kids ask questions, I lean in and receive each one as a gift. Their doubts are arrows pointing to the heart of the good Father, who has never shied away from hard questions. Instead, He came in person to answer them with a life lived as a sacrifice for every single kind of human who ever walked under the sun. The poor and the rich, the sinners and the wannabe saints, the hookers, the blind beggars, the mothers and the children who always pressed in hard to find a place in the sunshine of His voice and shared their lunches with Him.

So I break my naan bread and share my doubts with God at a table on an ordinary afternoon in Maryland, and the act of voicing my worries brings me closer to Him. The voice of wondering what I'm getting wrong and what I'm getting right and how I'm still afraid at the thought of dying young like my mom did brings me closer to Him. I'm full of the good food of being seen by a God who despises distance and comes to move into the neighborhood of my heart and replies to my hesitant syllables, drumbeat after drumbeat of loving me from the inside out.

I can feel how He likes me. Not the pretty version of me, although I'm sure He likes that part, too. But I feel how He likes me with my three-day hair and the jeans that are more comfortable with the top button undone. I feel Him leaning in and looking at that number on the scale and shrugging His shoulders and wrapping me in His affirmation. I hear His voice echo in my children's voices and in the paint night my friend is teaching at her mom's meet-up and in the group of middle school girls who meet with me on Tuesday afternoons to talk about friendship.

He isn't hindered by my rulers or insecurities. He is the God of the wide-open sky and the wide-open road, who comes running to meet His kids and knows each of us by name. Who loves us, and more than that, who *likes* us. This is the love story of the doubters who were always first called His friends.

It Was Hard to Believe
My Pastor on Sunday

*F*or the past few years it has become tradition for our family to spend Easter weekend in Pennsylvania with Jon and Christie at their farmhouse called Maplehurst. They're the friends who've known us the longest, since the days when none of us had kids yet.

Every year they host a neighborhood-wide two-thousand-plus Easter egg hunt. It is just as awesome as it sounds.

Our family stays on the third floor of their old farmhouse, and usually there are other guests in town too. A couple of years ago one of Christie's sisters, Kelli, and her four kids shared the third floor with us too. Or maybe it's better to say that we shared the floor with them.

Either way, I remember that weekend vividly. It was unseasonably warm. The tulips and daffodils were already in bloom. And long after everyone had left, we all lay on blankets in the front yard, surrounded by a sea of colorful empty plastic Easter eggs.

Kelli is a photographer and she captured the moment for us. She captured hundreds of beautiful moments that weekend. She was in transition herself, getting ready to move to Hawaii, where her marine husband was being stationed. I think we were all a bit jealous. Because Hawaii! And since her move, her Instagram feed has been a constant source of beauty, family, and inspiration from the sand and the sea.

But on Friday I got a text message from Christie that Kelli's husband, Shawn, was missing at sea. His helicopter and one other had gone down in the night and all twelve marines on board were still missing. A massive search spanning miles of ocean was launched.

On Sunday I was in a church service about how God can do the impossible.

Faith is so terribly hard, isn't it? Often mine comes accompanied by a large side of doubt and so many tears. Christie's brother and his wife are about to have a baby any day now, and Christie's first book, *Roots and Sky*, comes out in a week, but today she is headed to Hawaii to sit and wait with her sister and four kids for news no one wants to hear. This is what Christie wrote on her blog:

> It is likely that many of you will receive my book and begin
> reading it before I return home to Maplehurst. The only words
> I would add to the words already written within those pages are
> these:
>
> The book I wrote is not diminished by this sorrow. It is
> more true than I knew, and it has become, for me, an anchor
> outside this grief.
>
> It is, quite literally, the material form of my hope.
>
> If I once thought it was my gift to God then it is a gift he

has given back to me. I can hold hope in my hands, even if I fail to see it in these circumstances.*

I've cried and cleaned toilets since Friday. It seems easier than sitting still. How can one week ago look so different? And I spent several hours surrounded by unexpected family from home yesterday afternoon.

And that's the rub, isn't it? Amid all the darkness and the doubt and the crashing waves, there is still hope and light and family and new life. It's almost too hard to bear—all these contradictions that make up this life God has trusted us with.

How do we keep trusting Him back?

Maybe we just pray that He gives us eyes to see the rescue when it comes. Especially when it doesn't look like we expect.

So many are praying for Christie today as she flies with her oldest daughter to go be with her sister. Because that's what Christ has taught us, right? When things become too unbearable, when there are no words, we offer ourselves. Our presence. Like He taught us.

Emmanuel.

God with us. With you and with me and with Christie and with Kelli and with Shawn

---

* Christie Purifoy, "These Words Are Still True," *Christie Purifoy: A Spacious Place* (blog), January 17, 2016, www.christiepurifoy.com/2016/01/17/these-words-are-still-true. Used by permission.

My Faith Leaks

Sometimes on Monday mornings you can look up and find yourself in what feels like a tiny dinghy surrounded by vast waters. And those waters are choppy.

You get the kids off to school and you're running on time and in a good mood and then you have to walk back into your house. Or into your cubicle at work. Or into that classroom. And there are going to be bumps waiting for you. There are going to be people or news headlines or medical test results or phone calls from the school that make the water around you swell and sway and make you feel uneasy inside your little boat.

The headlines are loud these days, and the storm raging across this globe that we all call home can feel scary and desperate and as if there's no safe harbor to go to. Feelings are on the rise, as is the temperature of our political climate. On the weekends, I take refuge in stacks of laundry and cinnamon rolls for breakfast with the kids and a good book in the late afternoon.

The louder it gets in the world around us, the safer this ordinary house feels with its bathroom floors always covered with grit from the soccer fields and cleats left lying along the entrance-hall walls. I anchor myself to this house and its slow rhythm of Play-Doh parties and Xbox battles because here I know my name. And the people here know my name and they love me, with my hair that's long overdue for a cut and my jeans I've worn four days in a row.

But on Monday mornings those anchors go out into the world and I'm left alone with my thoughts and my work and the sometimes shouty emails and deadlines and I can start to feel like I'm sinking. I listen to the stories of my sisters that come to me like Morse code through Facebook and Twitter and text messages in chirps and hurts, and if we want to take our friendships to the next level, we have to lean in and resist the temptation to lean out when the conversations get hard.

Friendship is the long love letter of listening, even and especially when the conversations get uncomfortable. Open-palms conversations instead of clenched-fist accusations. Because this is what a body does—it asks the other parts if they hurt and then why and then, "What can we do?"

And then it listens.

And then it acts.

That will probably look different for each of us. But each of us will likely have a chance to act, to move closer toward friends in pain instead of putting distance between us, and that kind of action can change each of us.

I don't know exactly what that will look like for you. But I do know what happened a few years ago when a couple in our church shared with our small group that they were feeling desperate and frayed and financially stressed because their delivery business relied on having a car and their only car was broken down.

I remember clearly how the instant reaction from the group was to pray for them. And prayer is necessary. But sometimes what you really need is a loaner car. So while people moved forward to pray, the wife's eyes welled up with defeat, and my husband told me afterward that's when he knew that prayer in action looked like loaning them our second car. So he did.

And in that moment, we became a body instead of just a support group.

So what I'm saying is, I don't know the exact conversation God wants us all to have—you and me and our neighbors and the online spaces—but I do know that I want to go there together in a shared car. I want to talk about the things that ache in other parts of this body that Christ died for. I want to listen well. And after asking I want to get about doing.

And still, change is slow, and hurts can run deep, and I've looked around and wondered where Jesus is. Where is He in the headlines and deadlines and in our own families and sometimes even in our own bodies and definitely in our global church? Where is Jesus on the days when it feels as though He has fallen asleep on the job? I ask Him with all the arrogance of my stamped foot, my tiny mortal stamped foot that forgets itself and demands answers from its Creator.

Have you ever thought that?

Have you turned on the news and wondered what on earth is going on in the world today? With all its pain and conflict and fear and so much accusation and pointing fingers and deep hurt that there have been seasons I've stopped watching it altogether.

And Jesus? I don't know if I can trust Him, when I can't seem to find Him in all the loud shouting. It seems there's always something new to shout about, whether it's opposing opinions about refugees or air strikes or the terror unfolding in our schools. All the fear and the pointing fingers and the conversations I don't know how to have. I want to say things that help, and instead I end up taking naps because it's too much. I'm too little.

"I'm too little," I tell Him. "Where are You?" I demand. "Get up and help us already," I tell Him.

Because there are so many days that I can't make sense of this world He designed and that we have broken, and my faith feels like too little putty I'm trying to stuff into a crack in the bottom of my leaking boat. But the crack is too big for me, and my hands are too little, and my faith keeps letting the water seep in no matter how desperately I work to plug the holes in what I believe.

Wake up, Jesus. Wake up! Wake up! Wake up!

I'm saying these words in my head while we're getting ready for church. Air strikes have been launched overseas and I'm praying for my friends who have family in the military. And I'm praying for the organizations on the ground in the target country that have staff praying just as hard that they will escape being listed among any civilian casualties. So much at stake on so many sides, and every hurt voice haunts me. How do we begin to absorb it all, understand it all, empathize with it all? It's so impossible that it's immobilizing.

And then it hits me. The obvious. How did I miss it? I'm standing in front of the mirror with a curling iron in my hand when I remember that of course I'm not the first one.

Of course.

I'm not the first one to stand desperate in a boat, desperately afraid of the storm, wondering why in the world Jesus is asleep on the job.

Those first shaky disciples and I, we look out at the waves and the dark, angry clouds and we're so afraid of what's coming. We want to control it or outrun it or survive it. And all our faith is slipping through our fingers, and our boats are wobbly and our Savior is asleep.

I stood in front of the mirror and made myself remember the story.

Jesus wasn't asleep because He didn't care.

He was asleep because He wasn't afraid.

This is the part where my throat starts to get choked up and I put down the curling iron and just stare into space. And I can see two strong hands cover mine as I scrabble at the bottom of my leaky boat. Two hands that cover mine and cover the leak and I'm not in a little boat anymore; I'm standing on the solid ground of a wooden floor constructed by a trustworthy Carpenter.

I can't tell you exactly how I got there. I just know that Jesus doesn't merely plug holes; He builds floors. And bridges. And they stretch for mile after trustworthy mile. You can jump up and down on them. You can let your kids ride their bikes and their scooters on them with all the neighborhood kids. You can make your bed on them and you can picnic in the very center where the beams connect, groove to groove, in pools of sunshine.

I don't have easy answers to the hard questions, whether they're on the news or coming from your doctor or your kid's teacher or your coworker or a dear friend. I have only the hope of a hand in mine. The hand of this man, Jesus, who isn't afraid and who builds things that don't sink. Especially on Mondays.

So I take Him by the word and the hand and I take deliberate steps out of the familiar and onto the invitation built by His own example of putting His actions where His mouth was. He didn't just talk about loving us, delivering us, rescuing us; He up and left home and moved into the neighborhood. He stepped into our skins and our stories so that He could understand us, relate to us, connect with us from the inside out, literally.

I sit at our wooden farmhouse table with all the bread crumbs trapped in its grooves and I have tea with friends. We pass the milk and the sugar and sip the hot sweet flavor as we tell our stories, our fears, our worries, our hurts, and in turn we each receive like a gift what the others have said. To be trusted with someone's inner monologue is to be given a key to unlock a level of friendship not yet opened before.

We talk and of course we also laugh and we discover all the places our lives intersect and also all the spots where we need to keep learning from each other. Our small group is made up of women with roots in the Philippines, Tanzania, Germany, South Africa, El Salvador, Nicaragua, California, and Ohio. And every other Tuesday night, we grow closer as we overlap our lives and our time and our vulnerability to give and receive pieces of each other's stories. I hold all this trust like so much treasure in my hands. Along with the plate piled high from our eclectic potluck.

And this is the only way I know to quiet the storm of headlines that can paralyze me—to keep opening my door and inviting flesh-and-blood stories to come and sit and share around a table, one by one, so we can actually hear each other. To say yes to opportunities to be uncomfortable and say no to opening my mouth when what I need to do is be willing to linger in the words of someone else instead of rushing to have my own say.

So we keep laughing and sharing and sometimes aching together for all the times we got it wrong. But we don't give up the hope of wholeness, of believing that in our right-here-right-now lives we can actually take Christ up on His challenge to love because He first loved us. This can be hard when we're so deeply accustomed to defending ourselves and our points of view. We're skilled at putting up arguments and justifications that build walls and keep neighbors out.

But I am supposed to love my neighbor as myself (see Mark 12:31).

And "myself" desperately wants to be heard and understood. It's a kind of radical self-sacrifice, being willing to lay down my own point of view in order to hear someone else's. Jesus tells us,

> Self-help is no help at all. Self-sacrifice is the way, my way, to finding yourself, your true self. What kind of deal is it to get everything you want but lose yourself? What could you ever trade your soul for? (Matthew 16:24–26, MSG)

Love is a serious thing. It makes us blood family with Jesus. And He tells us exactly what that looks like. In John 13:34, He commands, "Love one another. As I have loved you, so you must love one another." Period.

Love always makes the first move. Because God so *loved* the world, He *sent* His only Son. And being willing to listen with hands open and fists unclenched is a radical act of love. This daring verb that is so much more than a date on the calendar or an ornament on a tree or a card or a gift or a word.

This word that makes us all family.

This word that builds bridges and plugs the holes in leaky boats.

Life and Grace

*M*y daughter comes to find me one Sunday morning in the bathroom. I'm just out of the shower, a towel wrapped around my middle, blow-drying my hair. I don't even think I have my contact lenses in yet when she asks me her question. It is a serious question and she seriously offers me this gift of trusting me with her truth. "Mom," she says, "I'm not sure I believe God is real."

I put down the dryer and pick up the brush and start sorting out the tangles. But I stop when I see her face, how serious she is. I stop and get down on my knees in front of her. This is sacred ground, talking about the things that matter to us, the things we believe and the things we're not sure yet how to believe. Because what if they let us down?

So I kneel and look into the deep ocean of her eyes and I take her question seriously. She elaborates, "Sometimes I think Jesus is real and I believe it. But then sometimes I worry it's just something my mind has made up and He's not really real."

Yes, I nod my head. Yes, this is familiar to me.

I hold both her hands and I can tell she's worried by what she thinks and by saying it out loud. There's so much power in words. We can speak whole worlds into existence. We can dig vast valleys between one another with our words or wade in really close, as close as DNA to DNA, when we are willing to speak the words that build bridges.

"I know what you mean," I tell her.

But I read on her face that she doesn't think I could possibly know. She thinks that all these years I've lived have made me sure of myself and certain of my faith. Instead, the only thing I'm sure of is that faith is being sure of what we cannot see.

"Zoe, I do know what you mean," I say. "There are days when I believe in every tiny part of my body that Jesus is real, and there are other days when I think that what we believe is a very strange story and I wonder how it all started."

She nods. And she repeats with emphasis, "But what if I just made it all up in my mind and God isn't really real?"

This is a question with weight to it: all the weight of the universe.

What if we believed that someone had been sent to pay the ransom and then that someone never actually came? What if we are all sitting here tied up in the dark waiting for rescue without being able to see that the road is empty and no one is coming?

Similar thoughts hold me hostage, too. But I've lived more years and I have more stories to offer her. So we kneel together on the bathroom mat, my hair wet and the towel tucked around me, and I remind her about the story I grew up in. The one where my mom died and my father scared me, and I ask her if she's scared of her oupa now. She isn't; she shakes her head. She loves him.

"Yes," I tell her. "He is different now. I don't know how to explain how different he is if I didn't believe in a God who changed him from the inside out." She's listening with her whole face.

"What about me?" I ask her. "What about this mother of yours who grew up thinking she didn't ever want to have kids? That having children would be a disappointment?"

I know she doesn't like this part of the story.

"But listen," I tell her, "having you three has been the best part of my story. The very best. And it's because I believe in a God who wanted me to understand that being a mom was a gift. He was never mad at me for not wanting kids. He wanted to make sure I knew how much He loved me just the way I was. He sent many people to tell me that. Your dad was one of them. So today I can sit here and hold you on my lap because I believe in a God who saved you like a surprise gift to give me."

She's still not convinced, but that's okay. It's not my job to convince her; it's my job to love her and keep inviting her into my story, which overlaps with her story. Because if this God I doubt and love, sometimes in the same breath, is real, then He will woo her gently and tenderly in His own way and in her own time with words that make sense to her.

I sit and brush her hair and stroke one finger down her soft cheek, and the next morning she'll wake up in bed next to me because she had a bad dream. And we'll be lying back to back and I'll roll over and tickle her arm gently to wake her up for school. Her eyes won't be open yet and I'll ask her how she slept, if her dream went away. "Yes," she'll say, "after I told it to you."

And I'll hug her and tell her that once she'd fallen back asleep I lay awake fighting back my own bad dreams. And without hesitation, without pausing for breath or planning what she's going to say or doubting what she believes, she will simply reach up and take my hand and pray with the conviction of the young, "Dear Lord, I pray for Mom. I pray You take away that bad dream and You let her know how much You love her. I pray You take all the bad thoughts out of her mind and only let her think about good things. Amen."

Just like that. Just like breathing. She prays over me, her mother. Her sister. Her fellow doubter and believer. We lie together under the sheets and we are the same, she and I. We want to believe beyond our doubts in one breath, and with the very next we pray to the God who can help our unbelief. And then we say, "Amen. Let it be so." And we walk down the hallway to get dressed and eat breakfast.

Another new day.

The gift of life and grace.

When You Wonder
If You Matter At All

*T*here were two years in South Africa that were both the worst and most wonderful of my life. The hard stuff made it easy to stay home on Sundays and get lost in a book or a TV show instead of a church service. Because there was always this lingering sense of showing up in a place where everyone else seemed to have it together, where everyone else was welcome, and where we just felt lost.

One Sunday, my fantastic stepmom, Wanda, announced I was going to church. She would watch baby Jackson, and my dad and husband and I would head to church. Honestly, the only part of that suggestion that was appealing to me was the thought of two whole hours without a demanding, crying baby. I would have gone just about anywhere for that kind of break.

We walked in and the place was packed. At the time, my parents' church was meeting in a high school auditorium. There was the wooden stage in front and the long hall-like room it looked out over. Hundreds of folding chairs lined the place from side to side and the band was already warming up onstage.

I sat down while everyone else around me was excitedly, happily hugging and greeting one another. I sat down and looked at my feet. I sat down lost and completely disassociated from the faith that used to come so naturally to me. I sat down and didn't feel anything.

And then I looked up and saw Jesus.

I mean, as clearly as the eye of your heart can show you something, I just knew He was up there on that stage standing behind, of all things, the ultra-hip band members (who had always intimidated me) as they tuned their instruments. I realize how wild it sounds, but all I can tell you is what I knew in that moment, what the Spirit showed me deep down in my wildly pounding heart. I could hardly swallow, the blood was ringing in my ears, and I knew for certain that Jesus was real and that He was looking at me.

He looked into my lonely, desperate self, and His face broke out into this wild, crazy-glad grin. And then He just leaped right off that stage and came running toward me, sweeping chairs and music stands out of His way and yelling over and over again, "You came! Oh, you came! I'm so *happy* you came!"

And then He was right there in front of my row, grabbing me off my feet and hugging me like a lunatic and jumping and dancing in glee and whooping, "I'm so happy you came! I'm *so* glad!" And something as hard as lead in my heart cracked and melted into the deep assurance that He loved me, just as I was. He loved me, He loved me, He loved me.

Even when I didn't feel lovable.

I'll never forget. I'll never forget His unbridled excitement that I had come to spend time in His Father's house. That I had brought my sadness and confusion home. And He didn't even bother mentioning any of that; He was too thrilled just to be together.

And in that moment, none of the questions I had for Him mattered. In that moment, there was just the joy of being wanted and the sense of belonging no matter how displaced my circumstances were. And it felt like a hug from a long-lost friend.

It's been a while since I thought about that night—twelve years since it took place. But last week a friend reminded me of that story and it all came back and I stood there with this goofy grin on my face, remembering the God who will leap chairs, hymnals, and anything else between us and Him to get His hands on us and His arms wrapped tightly around us.

I thought there might be someone else who needed to know that. Someone like me. Someone lost and lonely and in the middle and desperate for answers. I could try to give you those. But better yet I can tell you with absolute certainty that there is a God who is buck wild about you. And He *is* the answer. You don't need to produce or prove or practice or preach or perfect anything about your life.

All you have to do is show up. At church, in the laundry room, or locked behind the bathroom door. At the kitchen sink or when you're soaking in a bathtub or crying in the shower. Whether you're at the sidelines of another sports practice or sitting outside the grocery store for those stolen fifteen minutes of alone time. Whether your life is a tangled mess or you're in a season of beauty or peace or crushing anxiety. Whether you're in the middle of the middle, the beginning of the middle, or the very tired end.

Just go, ready to meet Him, and let Him do the rest. Because He will. Because He is a God who has been known to throw caution, dignity, and decorum to the wind and *run* toward His kids. He will come running for you, sister. He's already halfway toward you. All you have to do is look up and see Him.

When [she] was still a long way off, [her] father saw [her]. His heart pounding, he ran out, embraced [her], and kissed [her]. The [daughter] started [her] speech: "Father, I've sinned against God, I've sinned before you; I don't deserve to be called your [daughter] ever again."

But the father wasn't listening. He was calling to the servants, "Quick. Bring a clean set of clothes and dress [her]. Put the family ring on [her] finger and sandals on [her] feet. Then get a grain-fed heifer and roast it. We're going to feast! We're going to have a wonderful time! My [daughter] is here— given up for dead and now alive! Given up for lost and now found!" *And they began to have a wonderful time.* (Luke 15:20–24, MSG)

I've made that journey home, sister. More than once. And not one time did I regret it. Go home. You have a Father already running out to meet you.

Note to Self

I had to remind myself of a few things this morning: Even a run-walk is better than no run. You don't need the right workout clothes to work out. Your kids are not the boss of your feelings. God loves you because of who you are, not what you do. The forties are the love story of life in the middle—in the middle of kids, faith, doubt, marriage, failure, wonder, and the muffin top. And these are all good things.

I took the two youngest kids to the bus stop while dressed in leggings and my favorite T-shirt, which reads, "I'm just a sweatpants girl living in a skinny-jeans world." They try to teach me that dance move called flossing. It does not go well. But it's fun and also funny to try to get my hips and arms to move in opposite directions. I'm sure the bus driver finds it just as amusing when she pulls up. Zoe has a baggie of backup chocolate chip pancakes she's brought with her from the breakfast table. Girlfriend likes to be prepared and I admire that. Micah's hair is meticulously styled, and I know from experience it will all have fallen flat by the time he gets home. But they're both game for today and for the wonder of this ordinary Thursday and they board the bus with all my hopes and amazement stuffed into their backpacks, alongside the homework folders and the Chapstick they take everywhere.

I'm the mom on the corner waving and flossing to their embarrassed delight as the bus rumbles around the corner. Then I put in my earbuds and start my morning walk. I'm not good at routines or consistency, so this is only day two of this new attempt to keep this body that carries all my memories and all my future moving. But I embrace it with all the full throttle, full volume of my playlist. Maybe a forty-four-year-old mom shouldn't find so much joy in the pop tunes of a whole generation behind her, but there I go anyway, laughing and walking and dancing in my heart as I listen to Sadie Robertson and Anthem Lights belt out, "Don't let anybody take your tune. . . . You're original so just be you."*

The horses in the field I walk by raise lazy heads to glance in my direction and I walk close enough to smell their earthy scent wafted down the field of dandelions and sugary pop tunes as I kick at the road, wearing the Chucks that weren't ever intended for serious exercise. But I hold my head up and keep walking and I'm serenading this day, this life, that is so thick with both pollen and completely ordinary glory. I drive this road every day, infinity times a day, it seems, but somehow walking it slows me down and helps me see better.

There's the half-pipe the neighbors tried to build and that now they're dismantling for reasons I don't know, but I've enjoyed watching the story unfold out there on the side of the road. There's the new development and the new houses that I didn't know two years ago would be home to new friends who have sat around my table and sipped my tea

---

* Anthem Lights, "Just Be You," *Class of 2018*, featuring Sadie Robertson, copyright © 2017, Wavy Records/The Fuel Music.

and told me about what it's like to track the trajectory of a satellite or a friendship.

I walk and feel the weight of my body that no scale could properly measure, what the ancient text carved onto my mom's tombstone calls "an eternal weight of glory beyond all comparison" that far outweighs all our troubles (2 Corinthians 4:17, ESV). I'm learning to see, because I can feel it—how these days and roads and stories and moments are weighed down with the kind of ordinary wonder that will take your breath away more than a good run, more than that raise or praise or all those accolades.

As my friend Elise reminds me over and over again, this, *this*, is wealth. It will be there at 3:50 p.m., when my youngest two get off the bus again. It will be there at 4:30 p.m., when I pick up my teenager, who looks at me like I'm the exact kind of crazy fool I'm acting when I force him to listen to the hit songs from my own middle and high school years. I'll dance from the front seat and drive and laugh as I watch his eyes crinkle behind his glasses in horror and then fascination and then delight as he sees his mom as a woman who was once a girl who also thought she was all that and had the music to prove it.

I walk, and the road curves and beckons and bears witness, as I learn to love my own curves, as I enjoy them and exercise them and ask them to keep carrying me home. I don't want to outrun this season; I want to actually walk one step at a time right into it so I can take photos with my mind to store in my pocket for the days there aren't a million more miles of car pool waiting for me as there are still this afternoon.

Peter calls my cell phone as I turn onto our quiet, quirky little street and I'm taking a shortcut across our neighbor John's property. So I sit myself down on his Adirondack chairs next to his leaf-burning pit and

I cup my ear to the phone and hear my husband ask me about my morning so far. He is making his daily hour-long commute into the city after dropping off our oldest. I sit and swat bugs off my pants and lean in to catch his fascination as he updates me on stories of our boys from last night's baseball game that unfolded while I was at the elementary school art show. We swap stories about our new teenager and we laugh and plan how to outsmart him, or maybe it will just come down to our determination to out-love him.

The grass is yellow with dandelions, and puffs of whisper-soft seeds blow past me along with my laughter as I talk to the man who has been the main character in my story for more than two decades now. The air is fresh with spring and hope, and this season is the most ordinary un-ordinary I can remember. I'm old enough to recognize it and realize that no one can do this family just like we can. Because this is our story and we may sing out of key, but we like it that way and just keep singing louder together so that this music will echo off the walls and the years, and the ceiling won't be enough to hold in all the wonder that we have learned to see in one another. In a new pair of baseball cleats, in a fresh haircut, in the disappointment of the first football practice of the season that didn't go as hoped for but simply motivates us to push harder, be-friend more deliberately, suit up more determinedly next Sunday.

The teammates and classmates and playdates and dance parties that happen in the living room are like coming home over and over again, and the front door never gets tired of opening. Peter and I plan schedules and expectations for the weekend and then I hang up and walk the rest of the way home. The sun is still shining when the rain starts to chuckle down on me, cheeky drops that aren't serious about sticking around, just enough to make me laugh at the sun still shining through the water. My mom used to call days like this a monkey's wedding, and I have no idea what that nonsense saying means, except that now each of my kids says it too. Because this is our story and we inherited it from two different countries and we've made it a home now in our own house with the blue front door. I walk inside as cats chase me, hoping for breakfast.

The room is quiet, but I can still hear the echoes from this morning's laughter and yells to "get your things together quick, quick right now so we don't miss the bus." The dining room table has crumbs crushed deep and thick between the planks, and I get a small knife to slide them out and then pick up a paper towel to wipe them away and capture them in my hand. These bread crumbs and chip bits and traces of chalk and crayons and scraps of paper and glitter. I cup them in my hands, these tiny testimonies to the lives that live in this house.

And if I didn't know better, if I weren't looking, if I didn't have practice now living here in the very thick of the middle—me and my muffin top and the crumbs from this one glorious life—I might still believe that all this was ordinary.

With Thanks

In so many ways, this book is a love letter to people and to food. Here in the middle, both have become my favorite. Combine them and you've got a smorgasbord of what I imagine heaven might be like: conversation, connection, sugar, and carbs. There have been many kitchens and tables and plates and people and hours spent together, and I'm delighted I could celebrate so many of them in this book. And here now at the end are a few special thanks to the folks who helped me bring all these stories to life.

Jesus: Thank You for coming running for me when I was just six years old. From the upstairs window of an old house in Pennsylvania, I lifted my eyes to the hills for the first time, wondering where my help would come from, and I literally expected to see You. And I've believed in You ever since. Help me not to grow tired with the watching and the waiting. I pray that when I see You coming, I'll already be running hard in Your direction.

Peter: We will never forget this middle—this crossing over from the beginning to what comes next. As hard as some days have been, I'm glad I'm still holding your hand, which is still comfortingly so much bigger than mine, as we make the journey.

Jackson: Wednesday nights are the best gift you ever gave our family. Thank you for how you keep letting me into your life. Watching you become the grown-up version of yourself is the most fun no one told me to expect. I love that we can now share books, movies, and music. Yes, even some of my eighties music. You know that's right!

Micah: Thank you for being my living, breathing, hard-hugging, brave reminder that there is no one like our God and that we can never imagine what He has in store for us. I'm so grateful you came crashing into my life. You teach me about being brave, working hard, and answering curious questions. I cannot imagine my story without a Micah in it.

Zoe: Thank you for being my little mama. Your love is so generous and your friendship so unexpected that I will never get tired of listening to you tell me all your stories or being wrapped in your tight hugs or watching you with your new haircut or how you make art out of cardboard boxes. Thank you for how hard you love me, Zoe.

Jon and Christie Purifoy: From a handful of seeds and a pitcher of water to a sprawling garden, a podcast, a black barn, and seven kids between us! Thank you for being our friends who have dreamed dreams with us and been willing to also do the hard work of planting, watering, and harvesting. We are so grateful that we wandered into your home group on that cold Chicago night two decades ago. We pray we will all still be neighbors for all the next decades, too.

Amy Hinman: For all the hours spent doing everyday life together between daughters and chickens and Sunday school and "she sheds" and tea parties and faith. Your friendship has been soul food in this season.

The Rous and Baker families: For always loving us, praying for us, and championing us no matter the season, situation, or time zone.

Bethel Church: Thank you for being family to us.

Lily Myers: For her slam poem "Shrinking Women," stunningly performed at the 2013 College Unions Poetry Slam Invitational at Barnard College. Winner of the judges' award for Best Love Poem and eye-opening reminder to me and women everywhere that to love and nourish our bodies is to love and nourish our daughters.

Tina Constable: Thank you for being such an enthusiastic champion of this book, its readers, and its joyful cover. Having a publisher care so much has meant so very much.

Susan Tjaden: For turning my passion project into your passion project. And for letting so much of my quirky syntax slide. I'm so grateful to partner with an editor so enthusiastic and so kind.

Lisa Jackson: Remember when we sat in that empty cafeteria together and you told me I was allowed to write a collection of stories? That maybe I was actually called to do it? Thank you so much for being my agent and my friend and believing this would be a book even before I did.

OUT of **ORDINARY**
the

Lisa-Jo
Baker

Christie
Purifoy

Welcome to Out of the Ordinary, the podcast for anyone who's ever felt the nagging frustration of wondering if her life is too small, too boring, or too ordinary to make a difference. Join longtime friends and best-selling authors **Lisa-Jo Baker** and **Christie Purifoy** as they explore the surprising ways that cultivating ordinary life leads to extraordinary stories.

www.outoftheordinarypodcast.com

Lisa-Jo Baker is a champion and cheerleader for women who are longing for connection over perfection and for a big sister instead of a critic. In the past decade she has invited a highly engaged community of women into her completely ordinary life with humor, honesty, and camaraderie through her blog, social media, and in real life at events across the country.

She is the author of the best-selling *Never Unfriended* and *Surprised by Motherhood*, as well as *We Saved You a Seat* Bible study and its companion version for teen girls. She still considers connecting with women in real life the best part of her job. But this doesn't stop Netflix from being one of her BFFs.

Her writings have resonated with thousands and have been syndicated from New Zealand to New York, including on Huffington Post Parents, Bible Gateway, Fox News, BlogHer, *Deseret News, Christianity Today,* IF Table, *Reader's Digest,* Stroller Traffic, iVillage, OH Baby!, the Power of Moms, and Christianity.com.

She lives just outside Washington, DC, with her husband and their three very loud kids, where she spends hours every day driving her kids to sports practices and curling up at night with a good movie and a hot cup of tea with milk and sugar. She'd love to connect with you on Instagram @lisajobaker

To bring her to speak at your next event visit: www.lisajobaker.com/speaking

For everything you never expected about being a mom, read Lisa-Jo Baker's memoir

Before she arrived at the muffin-top middle, Lisa-Jo was stumbling through the sleep-deprived beginning of new motherhood. *Surprised by Motherhood* is her journey from South Africa to the United States and from swearing she would never be a mother to raising three of the loudest kids she knows. *The Middle Matters* is in so many ways the sequel to *Surprised by Motherhood*.